access to history

Italy: The Rise of Fascism 1915–45 THIRD EDITION

access to history

Italy: The Rise of Fascism 1915–45 THIRD EDITION

Mark Robson

Hodder Murray

A MEMBER OF THE HODDER HEADLINE GROUP

The publishers would like to thank the following individuals, institutions and companies for permission to reproduce copyright illustrations in this book:
© Alinari Archives/CORBIS, page 6; © Bettmann/CORBIS, pages 10, 27, 37, 59, 103, 121; © CORBIS, pages 122, 139; Getty Images, pages 22, 25, 30; © Hulton-Deutsch Collection/CORBIS, pages 28, 35, 104, 141; © Popperfoto.com, pages 89, 90; Solo Syndication/Associated Newspapers, page 118; Topham Picturepoint, page 58; © Underwood & Underwood/CORBIS, pages 46, 134.

The publishers would also like to thank the following for permission to reproduce material in this book:
AQA material is reproduced by permission of the Assessment and Qualification Alliance, used on page 40; Edexcel Limited for extracts used on page 53; Oxford, Cambridge and RSA (OCR) examinations for extracts used on pages 43, 79, 142.

The publishers would like to acknowledge use of the following extracts:
Cambridge University Press for extracts from *Mussolini Unleashed* by M. Knox, 1982; Random House Group Ltd for extracts from *Rise and Fall of the Third Reich* by W.L. Shirer, Martin Secker and Warburg, 1960.

Every effort has been made to trace all copyright holders, but if any have been inadvertently overlooked the Publishers will be pleased to make the necessary arrangements at the first opportunity.

Although every effort has been made to ensure that website addresses are correct at time of going to press, Hodder Murray cannot be held responsible for the content of any website mentioned in this book. It is sometimes possible to find a relocated web page by typing in the address of the home page for a website in the URL window of your browser.

Orders: please contact Bookpoint Ltd, 130 Milton Park, Abingdon, Oxon OX14 4SB. Telephone: (44) 01235 827720. Fax: (44) 01235 400454. Lines are open 9.00–5.00, Monday to Saturday, with a 24-hour message answering service. Visit our website at www.hoddereducation.co.uk

© Mark Robson 2006
First published in 2006 by
Hodder Murray, an imprint of Hodder Education,
a member of the Hodder Headline Group
338 Euston Road
London NW1 3BH

Impression number   10 9 8 7 6 5 4 3 2
Year   2010 2009 2008 2007 2006

The front cover shows Italian dictator Benito Mussolini as he returns from Munich in 1938 applauded as 'the Saviour of Peace'. © Mary Evans Picture Library.

Typeset in Baskerville 10/12pt and produced by Gray Publishing, Tunbridge Wells
Printed in Malta

A catalogue record for this title is available from the British Library.

ISBN-10: 0 340 90706 1
ISBN-13: 978 0 340 90706 1

Contents

Dedication

Keith Randell (1943–2002)

The *Access to History* series was conceived and developed by Keith, who created a series to 'cater for students as they are, not as we might wish them to be'. He leaves a living legacy of a series that for over 20 years has provided a trusted, stimulating and well-loved accompaniment to post-16 study. Our aim with these new editions is to continue to offer students the best possible support for their studies.

1 The Death of Benito Mussolini

On 25 April 1945 Benito Mussolini, the **Duce** of Fascism, the leader of Italy for two decades, was informed that German forces in Italy had surrendered to the advancing British and American armies. His allies and protectors had abandoned him and now he would have to face the vengeance of his fellow-countrymen. Angry, but defiant, he declared that he and 3000 loyal **blackshirts** would continue the war from the mountains of northern Italy.

Leaving Milan with a small band of followers and accompanied by his German SS bodyguard, he headed for the lakeside town of Como, intending to meet up with a much larger force of loyal Fascists. Arriving in Como on the evening of 25 April, the dictator could find no trace of these blackshirts. He moved on along the lakeside and then headed up the mountainside to the small village of Grandola. Here, at last, he found the main body of the Fascist forces. The *Duce* wanted to know how many men he now had at his disposal. Receiving no answer from the blackshirt commander he asked again,

'Well, tell me. How many?'
'Twelve', came the embarrassed reply.

Whatever illusions the *Duce* still had were shattered. The man who had once boasted of possessing an army of 'eight million bayonets' and an airforce large enough to 'blot out the sun', the leader who had once claimed to have the support of over 95 per cent of Italians was left with no more than a dozen supporters.

With all hope lost, Mussolini was persuaded to join a German convoy heading towards the Austrian border. Donning a German helmet and overcoat he tried to disguise himself. A few miles further on a group of partisans – Italian anti-Fascist resistance fighters – halted the convoy and searched it. Peering into the back of a truck a partisan spotted a hunched figure:

'Aren't you an Italian?', he demanded.
Mussolini paused then replied: 'Yes, I am an Italian.'
'Excellency', the man exclaimed, 'You are here!'

Recovering himself, the partisan arrested the former dictator and his mistress, Clara Petacci, and took them to a small farmhouse.

At about 4pm on 28 April a stranger burst into Mussolini's room calling out 'Hurry up, I've come to rescue you.' Taking them out of the house, he pushed Mussolini and his mistress into his waiting car and drove off. After a few minutes the car stopped and the couple were ordered out. Within seconds the *Duce* and Clara Petacci had been shot. Their executioner was a partisan authorised by his resistance group to kill the ex-dictator.

The bodies were put back into the car and then transferred to a removal van already loaded with the corpses of 15 Fascists. Mussolini's body was slung on the top of the pile. The following day his and his mistress's bodies, now mutilated, were hung upside down from a garage roof in Milan's Piazzale Loreto to be mocked by jeering crowds.

Such was the ignominious end of the man who had dominated Italy for 20 years, the man who had claimed to have invented Fascism, the man who had swept away the old Liberal regime, the man who had vowed to make his country 'great, respected and feared'.

The question of how Mussolini rose from obscurity to overthrow the Liberal system of government and create Europe's first Fascist dictatorship is the central theme of this book. To understand fully the rise of Fascism and the nature of the Fascist dictatorship, it is important to examine both the circumstances in which Italy became a united country in 1870 and the weaknesses of the Italian state in the years immediately prior to the First World War. These themes are examined in Chapter 2.

2 The Weaknesses of Liberal Italy 1870–1915

POINTS TO CONSIDER

Mussolini and his Fascists rose to power in the years immediately following the First World War, replacing the old Liberal regime. However, the rise of Fascism cannot be understood simply by examining the events from 1915 to 1922. This chapter considers the problems that faced Italy and its Liberal rulers immediately prior to the war, and shows that many of the factors which would help to cause the collapse of the Liberal regime in 1922 were already visible in the years leading up to Italian entry into the war in 1915. These problems and factors are addressed through the following themes:

- The unification of Italy 1815–70
- Problems facing Liberal Italy 1870–1915
- Liberal Italy on the eve of the First World War

Key dates

1859	Seizure of most of northern Italy by the Kingdom of Piedmont
1861	Seizure of southern and central Italy by the Kingdom of Piedmont, but with Rome remaining under the control of the Pope
	Kingdom of Italy established. King of Piedmont became first King of Italy
1870	Rome seized by Italian troops. Unification of Italy completed
1895	Italian Socialist Party founded
1911	Conquest of Libya expanded Italian Empire in Africa
1912	Universal male suffrage
1915	Italy joined First World War on the side of Britain and France

Key question
How did the unification of Italy come about?

1 | The Unification of Italy 1815–70

In 1815 Italy, as the Austrian statesman Metternich pointed out, was only 'a geographical expression'. The country had not known political union for about 1500 years. It was a collection of relatively small, often quarrelling states. In the past, there had been great wealth in cities such as Florence, Venice and Rome, together with impressive cultural achievements, but the country had rarely been free from war or foreign domination. Indeed, while the likes of Leonardo da Vinci and Michelangelo were creating their great works of art during the 'Italian Renaissance' of the fifteenth and sixteenth centuries, Italy had been the battleground of Europe, as French and Spanish armies fought for supremacy.

In 1815 the states of the Italian peninsula were, for the most part, politically **reactionary** and economically backward. The most determined reaction and abject poverty was to be found in the south, in the kingdom of the Two Sicilies. Central Italy was dominated by the Papal States, over which the Pope was not only the religious but also the political ruler. Further north were the small states of Tuscany, Modena, Parma, and the more economically advanced kingdom of Piedmont, based in Turin. The traditional foreign presence was provided by Austria, which occupied Lombardy and Venetia.

Risorgimento

The period after 1815 witnessed an Italian literary and cultural revival, the *Risorgimento*, literally 'resurgence' or 're-birth', which lamented Italian divisions and foreign domination, called for a new sense of Italian patriotism, and demanded the political unification of the country. This movement particularly attracted students and the small professional classes, principally in the north. The kingdom of Piedmont was, however, the driving force behind unification.

In 1859 the Piedmontese statesman, Camillo Cavour, won French support for his expansionist ambitions. French arms forced Austria to cede Lombardy to Piedmont, while Tuscany, Modena, Parma and the Papal State of the Romagna were persuaded to give up their independence and join the kingdom of Piedmont. In the same year, Garibaldi, the romantic adventurer and popular hero of the unification, invaded Sicily with 1000 armed men – his 'Red Shirts'. Despite the small size of his army, he had succeeded in conquering the kingdom of the Two Sicilies by late 1860. Garibaldi was then persuaded to hand over the state to King Victor Emmanuel II of Piedmont. At the same time a second part of the Papal States was annexed, leaving the Pope with only the area surrounding Rome.

In 1861 the kingdom of Italy was established as a **constitutional monarchy** based very closely on that of Piedmont. Italian support for Prussia in the Austro-Prussian war of 1866 led to the acquisition of Venetia from Austria. Finally in 1870, Rome, the last independent territory in the peninsula, fell to Italian troops after the French had removed their soldiers from protecting the Holy City to fight in the Franco-Prussian war.

Key term

Reactionary
Hostile to parliamentary or democratic government, dismissive of individual freedoms, deeply suspicious of change.

Key dates

Seizure of most of northern Italy by the Kingdom of Piedmont: 1859

Seizure of southern and central Italy by the kingdom of Piedmont, but with Rome remaining under the control of the Pope: 1861

Kingdom of Italy established. King of Piedmont became King of Italy: 1861

Rome seized by Italian troops. Unification of Italy completed: 1870

Key term

Constitutional monarchy
The King was the head of state but the Prime Minister was the head of the government. The King had the power to dismiss Prime Ministers but in practice left day-to-day politics in the hands of the Prime Minister and parliament. To stay in office and to pass new laws the Prime Minister needed the approval of the elected parliament.

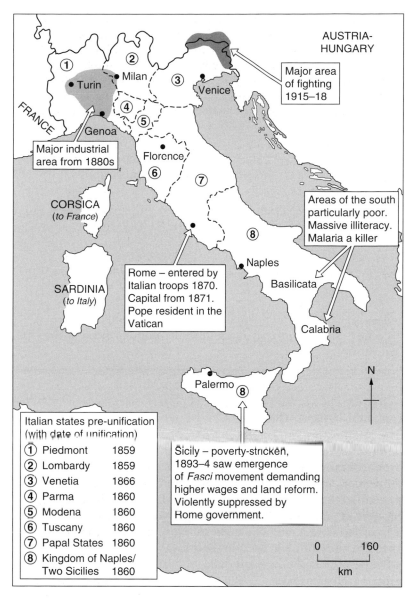

Italy: from unification to the First World War.

2 | Problems Facing Liberal Italy 1870–1915

Key question
How serious were the problems faced by the Liberal rulers of Italy?

The political unification of the states of the Italian peninsula was thus complete by 1870. With only two per cent of the population possessing the vote, the new state was to be dominated by the representatives of the wealthy and middle classes, and these were overwhelmingly Liberals. Liberals saw themselves as an educated élite who would lead Italy forward to national unity, economic prosperity and great power status. They were, however, to find formidable obstacles in their path.

Profile: Giuseppe Garibaldi 1807–82

1807	– Born in Nice, in the kingdom of Piedmont
1834	– Joined Young Italy movement dedicated to unification of Italy. Forced into exile, first in France then travelled to South America
1848	– Returned to Italy and fought in the unsuccessful attempt to overthrow the rule of the Pope in the Papal States
1859	– Fought for the kingdom of Piedmont in war to remove Austrian rule from much of northern Italy
1860	– Invaded Sicily with 1000 volunteers. Crossed to the mainland and seized Naples. Handed over his conquests to the kingdom of Piedmont
1866	– Served in the Austrian War
1870	– Fought for France in the Franco-Prussian War
1871	– Retired to island of Caprera, where he died 11 years later

Giuseppe Garibaldi's exploits, his charisma and his devotion to the cause of a united Italy made him the popular hero of the unification.

Lack of Italian identity

The long history of political division had done little to foster a sense of national identity among Italians. Only a very small proportion of Italians had played any role in bringing about unification and loyalties tended to be towards the family or the immediate locality rather than towards the Italian nation. To complicate matters, only about two per cent of the population actually spoke Italian. The great majority spoke dialects that were virtually unintelligible outside their local area. What was known as 'Italian' was simply the local dialect of Tuscany, the province centring on Florence.

Hostility of the Catholic Church

The Catholic Church was a powerful force in Italian society, claiming at least the nominal allegiance of the vast majority of the population, and it was bitterly resentful of the new kingdom of Italy that had seized the Papal States and Rome from the Church. In retaliation the Pope refused to recognise the Italian state and instructed loyal Catholics to boycott all elections. This ban was lifted in the 1890s but distrust between the Church and the Liberal regime remained a factor in Italian politics up to and beyond the First World War.

Economic weakness

Italy was still predominantly an agricultural country, with some 68 per cent of the population dependent on the land for at least part of their livelihood. Most peasants and farm labourers, particularly

Key terms

Two-party system
A political system, as in Britain, where there are two dominant and distinct parties who compete for power.

Trasformismo
Different political factions forming a coalition government regardless of ideological differences.

Socialist
Socialists argued that the existing political and economic systems of Europe oppressed the poor. Socialists worked to improve the political and economic status of the working class. Some believed the existing political systems could be reformed peacefully, others argued that only violent revolution could bring about meaningful change.

Key question
Why did the Liberals face growing challenges to their political dominance?

in the south, lived in poverty. Industry was also relatively undeveloped. Most enterprises were small scale, centring around workshops and skilled craftsmen. Heavy industry was at a disadvantage because of the lack of natural resources, principally coal and iron ore. There was some development in iron and steel and shipbuilding, but this was largely limited to military purposes and railways and was concentrated in the north.

Weaknesses of the Liberal political system

The parliamentary system had been partly based on the British model but in certain vital respects it was very different – there were no clearly defined political parties and there was no **two-party system**. As the urban and rural poor did not have the vote, politicians were drawn mainly from the professional, wealthy middle class and represented this narrow social class in parliament. These Liberals were not divided by ideology and, in fact, had relatively few major differences of opinion. Consequently, there seemed to be no necessity for formal political parties that might draw up policy, elect leaders and discipline dissenting members.

In the absence of well-organised parties, members of parliament, or deputies as they were known, clustered around prominent politicians and formed factions. A number of factions would agree to support each other and form a government, dividing up the ministerial posts between them. This was the politics of *Trasformismo*, where former political opponents might temporarily put aside their differences and come together in government. Of course, such alliances were fragile and when a leading politician felt aggrieved over an issue he would withdraw his faction's support and the government would fall. In fact, such was the turnover of governments that Italy had 29 Prime Ministers between 1870 and 1922.

To critics, these ever-changing governments indicated that Liberal politics was not about principle or the good of the nation, it was simply the pursuit of power for its own sake.

Growing challenges to Liberal political dominance

The political dominance of the Liberals was unchallenged for the first 20 years of the new Italian state, but from the 1890s three growing forces threatened the Liberals' monopoly of political power.

Socialism

Rapid industrialisation in northern Italy from the 1880s produced a sizeable working class who were attracted to **Socialist** ideas concerning pay, working conditions and the ownership of industry. A Liberal reform of 1881, allowing some two million more Italians to vote, provided an added incentive for Socialists to organise. The first determined attempt to create a single, united Socialist party was made by Filippo Turati, a middle class lawyer, when, in 1891, he organised an Italian Workers' Congress in Milan.

At the Genoa Congress of 1892 the movement divided into two broad groupings. The first dedicated itself to revolutionary strikes and refused to participate in elections or parliamentary politics. The second and larger group also committed itself to workers' control of the state, but realised that this must be a long-term aim. It argued that in the meantime, and to achieve this ultimate goal, Socialists should work to extract better pay and conditions from employers, and should involve themselves in local and national politics, even if this meant dealing with the hated Liberals.

Key date

Italian Socialist Party founded: 1895

This more moderate group, including Turati, became the Italian Socialist Party (PSI) in 1895. By 1897 it had 27,000 members and ran its own newspaper, *Avanti*. In 1900, it received over 200,000 votes in the general election and secured 32 seats in the chamber of deputies, the lower house of the Italian parliament. According to its manifesto, these deputies were resolved to demand the introduction of **universal manhood suffrage**, an eight-hour day, income tax and women's rights. But despite the fact that Socialism still had relatively little support by the turn of the century and had adopted a moderate programme, its emergence had provoked great fears. Such fears were particularly pronounced in the Catholic Church.

Catholicism

For the first decade or more after unification the Catholic Church focused its hostility on the Liberal regime, but by the 1890s the Papacy had turned its attention to the rise of Socialism. The Bishop of Verona told his parishioners:

> Socialism is the most abject slavery, it is flagrant injustice, it is the craziest folly, it is a social crime, it is the destruction of the family and of public welfare, it is the self-proclaimed and inevitable enemy of religion, and it leads to anarchy.

Key terms

Universal manhood suffrage
The right to vote for all men over the age of 21.

Anti-clericals
Those politicians, mainly Liberal, who opposed the claims of the Catholic Church that it deserved a privileged position within the Italian state.

To head off the danger of Socialist gains in parliament, the Church removed its ban on Catholics voting in general elections. By 1909 Catholics were even permitted to put themselves forward as candidates for election.

The Pope remained adamantly opposed to the formation of a Catholic political party that might rival his authority over the faithful, but the Catholics still presented a major challenge to the Liberal regime. Now that the Catholics were active participants in national politics, was it possible to ignore them, or must some form of accommodation be attempted? If there was to be a *rapprochement*, what would the terms be, and how could leading Liberals deal with the remaining **anti-clericals** in their own ranks?

Nationalism

Nationalists, often middle class intellectuals, were few in number but they found many supporters in the media. They accused Liberals of putting their own careers before the good of the country. In particular, they condemned the regime for failing to make Italy a great power, the equal of France or Britain. They demanded a larger Italian Empire in Africa and higher military spending. A more aggressive foreign policy, they argued, would help to forge an Italian nation and reinvigorate Italian politics. It would be the Nationalists who would lead the calls for Italian entry into the First World War and who would be an early influence on Fascism.

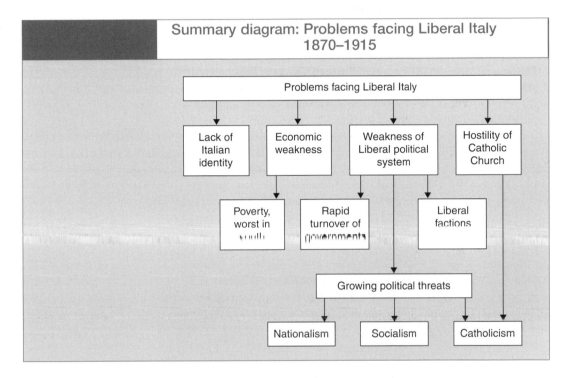

Summary diagram: Problems facing Liberal Italy 1870–1915

Key question
How stable was the Liberal regime in the years leading up to the First World War?

3 | Liberal Italy on the Eve of the First World War

The positive view

Liberals argued that Italy had made huge progress under their rule and that the country was evolving into a strong and healthy democracy in the years immediately prior to the First World War.

National military service and the introduction of free primary education had helped to create a greater sense of Italian nationhood. Economic progress had been rapid, as evidenced by national income rising from 61 billion lira in 1895 to 92 billion lira in 1915, and by a six-fold increase in foreign trade in the 50 years up to 1913. Taxes on food had been reduced, and Liberal governments had spent money to improve roads, railways and the supply of drinking water.

In the field of foreign affairs, Italy had joined the **Triple Alliance** with Germany and Austria-Hungary, and built up an empire in East Africa. The conquest of Libya in 1911 had confirmed Italy as a great power.

Most importantly, according to the Liberals, Italy had a robust, stable political system. The vote had been progressively extended so that from 1912 there was effectively universal male suffrage. The skilful Liberal leader Giovanni Giolitti, who was Prime Minister for all but three of the years 1903–14, had managed to co-opt both moderate Socialists and moderate Catholics into his governing coalition.

The regime was thus winning the support of the key groups within Italian society. The English historian, G.M. Trevelyan, writing in the years before the First World War, illustrated this positive view:

> Nothing is more remarkable than the stability of the Italian kingdom and the building is as safe as any in Europe. The foundations of human liberty and the foundations of social order exist there on a firm basis.

Liberal Prime Minister Giovanni Giolitti 1842–1928. Giolitti was Prime Minister on four occasions in the years 1903–14. He passed a number of reforms and was adept at forming majorities in Italian parliament. He was also Prime Minister in 1920–1 and offered Mussolini and his Fascists an electoral alliance in 1921.

Key term

Triple Alliance
Military alliance between Italy, Germany and Austria-Hungary signed in 1882.

Key dates

Conquest of Libya expanded Italian Empire in Africa: 1911

Universal male suffrage: 1912

The negative view

This rosy vision of a successful Liberal Italy was firmly rejected by the Liberals' political opponents.

Socialist criticisms of Liberal Italy

Socialists condemned the regime as a cover for capitalist exploitation of the Italian working classes. Their argument was as follows. Wages were still very low and hours were very long when compared with the rest of Western Europe. Welfare benefits, such as sickness and pension payments, also compared unfavourably. Any improvements in the life of the Italian worker had been wrung out of a state always too willing to use the army to crush strikers and opposing political groups. The wealth of the country had been squandered on imperialist adventures in East Africa and Libya. Severe poverty was still widespread. The fact that five million Italians had chosen to emigrate to the USA and South America in the period 1871–1915 confirmed the failure of Liberalism to address the problem of poverty, let alone to solve it. For the Socialists, the question was not whether the Liberal regime would collapse, but how soon, and what methods would bring it about.

Nationalist criticisms of Liberal Italy

To the Nationalists, the regime was equally contemptible. It had lacked the will to make Italy a major force on the European scene. Liberal incompetence had led to a humiliating military defeat at the hands of the Ethiopians in 1896. For Nationalists, the vast emigration was also a national disgrace. These emigrants were men and women whose energy should have been employed to build up the Italian economy and fill the ranks of its armies. Liberalism, through its weakness, had only exacerbated the struggle between classes. The state had neither crushed Socialism effectively, nor provided a relevant alternative creed for Italian workers to believe in. Liberalism had never instilled an Italian 'national spirit', not least because its politicians lacked all principle. They were only concerned about their own careers and private interests and they made deals with anyone who could further their selfish aims. Giolitti himself was the epitome of such a lack of belief in public service. He had allied with Socialists and Catholics and had shamelessly attempted to use the government's powers to manipulate the results of general elections.

Catholic criticisms of Liberal Italy

Catholics were divided over Liberalism. Many found it difficult to support a regime which in 1870 had trampled over the Pope's territorial rights in Rome. Furthermore, the introduction of the wider suffrage had encouraged the emergence of Catholic groups dedicated to helping the poor Catholic peasantry. Governments during the Giolittian era had granted monies to southern provinces to improve irrigation and the supply of drinking water, but the sums had proved woefully inadequate. Poverty remained a desperate problem, particularly in Sicily where 0.01 per cent of the population owned 50 per cent of the land, leaving a mass of landless peasants. From the late 1890s onwards southerners formed the majority of those 200,000 Italians emigrating overseas each year. This was proof of the seriousness of the 'southern problem'.

Catholic groups who looked towards social reform as a means of alleviating continuing poverty would form part of the Popular Party (the *Popolari*) established after the First World War and they were determined not to be absorbed into the Liberal system. For them, the Liberals represented an urban educated élite who had little interest in or understanding of the real Italy. On the other hand, more conservative Catholics saw the regime as infinitely preferable to Socialism. Liberalism might be far from ideal, but they feared that a Catholic political party in the hands of more radical reformers would be less willing than the Liberals to defend their property interests. In any case, the Pope was not yet prepared to permit the formation of a Catholic political party, a potential rival to his own authority.

Popolari
Catholic political party founded in January 1919.

Key term

Political divisions

The Liberal regime had certainly seen economic growth and introduced some social reform, but divisions within Italian society remained wide. Economic divisions were illustrated by the increasing contrast between the growing prosperity of the industrialising north and the abject poverty of the rural south. Social divisions were seen in industrial disputes between a growing urban working class and their middle class employers.

Most significant were the political divisions. Giolitti had temporarily managed to form a coalition of moderate Socialists, Catholics and Liberals, but the Libyan war of 1911 had blown this apart. The Socialist Party had condemned the war and revolutionaries displaced the moderate reformists as the dominant faction within the party. The Socialist newspaper, *Avanti*, edited by a young firebrand named Benito Mussolini, now called for the abolition of private property and advocated violent strikes to overthrow the state. The right was appalled, and many believed that Giolitti had been too conciliatory towards the Left. Such conservatives began to listen to those who condemned not just Giolitti, but the whole Liberal system. These Nationalists despised the manoeuvrings in parliament, accused the politicians of neglecting Italian interests, and demanded that Italy must be a truly 'great power'. In order to achieve this some form of **authoritarian state** would probably be necessary. The Nationalists secured few votes but their influence over conservative groups such as industrialists and landowners was out of all proportion to their numbers. Italian politics was **polarising**.

As the First World War broke out in Europe in 1914, the Liberals remained in power but their basis of support was shallow and, now that the vast majority of male Italians had the vote, Socialist and Catholic opponents were growing in strength. The Liberal regime was in no imminent danger of collapse, but it was clear that the Liberal monopoly of power was over. The test for

Authoritarian state
A state with a strong central government that is able and willing to ignore parliament and suppress dissent.

Polarising
Moving towards extremes.

Key terms

the Liberal political system was to see whether the practice of *Trasformismo* could bring moderate Catholics and Socialists into a Liberal coalition government, forming a new consensus which would narrow political divisions and marginalise the extremists – the revolutionary Socialists on the left and the Nationalists on the right. This, however, would be a very difficult task.

Liberal difficulties were exacerbated by the personal rivalries between Liberal leaders and divisions over whether to enter the war. For some Liberals a victorious war might finally unite their nation, create a new political consensus, and enable the Liberals to claim the credit for making Italy a 'great power'. In the event, when Italy did enter the war, in 1915, the effect was quite the opposite: the war widened political and social divisions still further, undermined Liberal prestige, and sowed the seeds for the growth of Fascism.

Key date

Italy entered the First World War: 1915

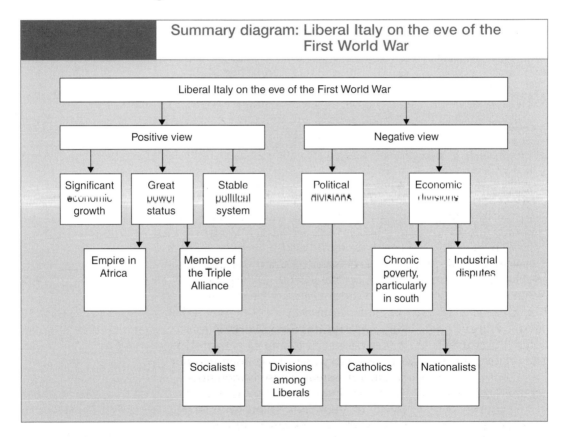

Summary diagram: Liberal Italy on the eve of the First World War

Liberal Italy on the eve of the First World War

Positive view / Negative view

Significant economic growth / Great power status / Stable political system / Political divisions / Economic divisions

Empire in Africa / Member of the Triple Alliance / Chronic poverty, particularly in south / Industrial disputes

Socialists / Divisions among Liberals / Catholics / Nationalists

3 The Rise of Fascism 1915–22

POINTS TO CONSIDER
Fascism was only founded as a political movement in 1919 and was insignificant until late in 1920. Nevertheless, by the end of October 1922, its leader, Benito Mussolini, had been appointed Prime Minister. Why did Fascism rise to prominence so quickly? How important was Mussolini to its success? How far were the First World War and its consequences responsible for the rise of Fascism? To what extent did Liberal failings enable the success of Fascism? This chapter addresses these key questions under the following headings:

- Italy at war
- The economic legacy of the First World War
- The Socialist 'threat'
- 'Mutilated victory'
- Mussolini and the birth of Fascism
- The rise of Fascism 1919–21
- Mussolini seizes the initiative: May 1921–October 1922
- The march on Rome

The final section of the chapter examines the historical debate surrounding the rise of Fascism.

Key dates

1915	May	Italy entered the First World War
1917	October	Italian defeat at Battle of Caporetto
1918	October	Italian victory at Vittorio Veneto caused Austria to sue for peace
1919	March	First meeting of Fascist movement
	June	Treaty of Versailles failed to award any German colonies to Italy
	September	Treaty of St Germain with Austria Seizure of Fiume by Nationalist Gabriele D'Annunzio
	November	First post-war general election. Socialists became largest party and Liberals could no longer rule alone. Fascists failed to win a single seat
1920	September	Occupation of the factories by 400,000 engineering workers
	November	Fascist squad violence began

1921	May	Fascists gained 35 seats in general election
	October	National Fascist Party organisation created
1922		Increasing Fascist violence
	July	Abortive Socialist general strike
	October 27	Fascists seized key buildings in northern cities, the first move in the planned 'March on Rome'
	28	Resignation of last Liberal government
	29	Mussolini invited to become Prime Minister
	30	Mussolini arrived in Rome. Fascists organised victory parade

1 | Italy at War

Key question
What did Italy hope to gain by joining the First World War?

In August 1914 the great powers of Europe went to war. However, Italy remained aloof. Her membership of the Triple Alliance apparently committed her to support Germany and Austria-Hungary, but the government in Rome now declared the Alliance defunct. It claimed that Austria had broken the terms of the treaty by attacking Serbia without consulting Italy, and by seeking to expand her empire into the Balkans.

The great majority of Italians welcomed this decision. In fact, many Italians possessed an underlying hostility towards Austria-Hungary, a country that had resisted Italian unification by force in the 1850s and 1860s, and which still occupied territories inhabited by Italian speakers, notably the Trentino and Istria (see the map on page 26).

Decision for war

Most Italians were satisfied with neutrality: some Liberals, including former Prime Minister Giolitti, together with most Catholics and Socialists, and much of the army and big business, believed either that Italy was not ready for war or that war would be bad for Italian society and the economy. However, Liberals supporting the Prime Minister, Antonio Salandra, had misgivings. They feared that victory for the Triple Alliance would only strengthen Austrian resistance to revision of its borders with Italy.

Key term
Entente powers
The Alliance of Britain, France and Russia (Triple Entente).

Alternatively, if the **Entente powers** won, they would not be sympathetic to Italian ambitions in the Mediterranean if Italy had done nothing to bring about their victory. The government increasingly took the view that Italy must intervene in the war at some point and should negotiate with both sides in order to obtain the best terms for joining either the Alliance or the Entente. This policy was encouraged by the noisy demands of the Nationalist press that Italy must grasp its chance to become a great power.

Key date
Italy entered the First World War: May 1915

Throughout the early months of 1915 negotiations continued. It became very apparent that, although Austria-Hungary would make some territorial concessions, these would not include the

Italian-speaking areas of the Trentino or the city of Trieste. In contrast, the Entente promised Italy that it would receive not only the Trentino and Trieste but also other Austrian lands in the southern Tyrol, Istria and Dalmatia (see the map on page 26). The Italian kingdom would then dominate the Adriatic Sea. There was also the promise of further colonies, as yet unspecified but probably in Africa or the eastern Mediterranean. Therefore, it was not surprising that, in May 1915, the government entered the First World War on the side of the Entente. It was a fateful decision. The war was to have traumatic consequences for Italy's society, economy and political system.

Italy at war

Although the decision to join the war was hailed by crowds of ecstatic Nationalists, Italian intervention did not fire the imagination of the mass of the population. It was hard, for example, for a poor southerner to be enthusiastic about fighting for a few Italian-speaking areas on the country's north-eastern frontier. Catholics were made aware that, although their Church was broadly supportive of the war effort, it would not actively denounce the enemy, Catholic Austria. Italian Socialists openly condemned the conflict as a capitalist or 'bosses'' war. Even some Liberals, grouped around Giolitti, attacked the decision to go to war.

Key question
Why did the conduct of the war lead to criticism of the Liberal regime?

Despite the absence of anything resembling war hysteria, five million men eventually served in the army, mainly as conscripts. Most of these conscripts came from rural areas, as much of the industrial working class was involved in producing war material and was therefore exempt from military service. The great majority of soldiers fought bravely, endured appalling conditions in the front line, and tolerated miserable rations and low pay. However, the expected victory did not materialise and, dogged by unimaginative leadership, the Italian army found itself in a murderous **war of attrition** on its Alpine northern border. The winter weather, the effect of stone splinters from the impact of high explosive shells, and the determination of many Italian commanders to maintain the offensive meant that casualties were heavy. On many occasions, thousands of lives were sacrificed in an attempt to gain a few hundred metres of mountainside.

Eventually, after two years of war, the Italian army cracked under a surprise Austro-German attack. At the Battle of Caporetto 700,000 Italians retreated in disorder for over 100 miles until the line was held at the river Piave. Around 300,000 Italians were taken prisoner. Recriminations abounded. Cadorna, the army's commander-in-chief, blamed the defeat on the supposed cowardice of the troops. He executed several thousand as retribution. Nationalists blamed the government for inefficiency in running the war and in supplying the troops. The government blamed Cadorna himself, and promptly sacked him.

Despite the arguments, the situation stabilised. As 1918 wore on, a shortage of food and munitions combined with general war-weariness to weaken the resolve of Austria-Hungary and Germany.

War of attrition
A war in which the commanders do not expect dramatic victories but instead measure success in terms of metres of territory gained and number of enemy killed.

Key term

Italy entered the First World War: May 1915

Italian defeat at Battle of Caporetto: October 1917

Key dates

Key term

Armistice
Agreement to cease fighting.

Key date

Italian victory at Vittorio Veneto caused Austria to sue for peace: October 1918

Key question
How did the First World War make the problems of Liberal Italy worse?

In October, as Germany reeled from an Anglo-French offensive, the Italian army attacked the Austrians. In the fighting that ensued, casualties were heavy on both sides, with the Italians losing nearly 40,000 men killed or wounded. Finally, the Austrian will to resist collapsed and the Italian forces found themselves in possession of about 500,000 prisoners of war. The victory, to be known as the Battle of Vittorio Veneto, caused Austria to sue for peace. An **armistice** was signed on 3 November 1918.

2 | The Economic Legacy of the First World War

The war ended with Caporetto avenged and the country looking forward to enjoying the fruits of victory. However, Italians were to be disappointed. The war had enhanced their country's claims to great power status, but the eagerly anticipated territorial gains only partly materialised. Furthermore, the war had left Italy with severe domestic problems which would widen existing social and political divisions.

Inflation

First, the human cost of the war had been enormous. A total of 650,000 men had died and one million more had been seriously wounded. In addition, the financial cost of keeping the soldiers armed and fed had placed a heavy burden on the Italian treasury. Huge sums had been borrowed from Britain and the USA – the national debt had increased from 16 billion lira in 1914 to 85 billion lira in 1919. However, these borrowings had proved inadequate to pay for the war and the government had resorted to printing money. This had a dramatic effect. Inflation spiralled as ever greater quantities of paper money chased ever scarcer goods. Prices quadrupled during the war years.

Inflation destroyed savings, hitting the middle classes in particular. Landowners relying on rents and state employees whose wages did not keep up with increasing prices also suffered. Nor did factory workers escape. The purchasing power of their wages fell by about 25 per cent between 1915 and 1918.

Industrialists, in contrast, did well out of the war. Providing their production was linked to the war effort, they were assured of a market. As inflation increased they simply raised their prices and a government desperate for military victory continued to buy their products. Large companies such as Pirelli tyres and Montecatini chemicals made huge profits while Fiat expanded to the point where it became the largest manufacturer of commercial vehicles in Europe in 1918. However, victory meant the end of easy profits. There was no longer any need for enormous quantities of rifles, artillery, trucks and the like. A government which, in 1918, had spent 23.3 billion lira more than it had collected in taxes could no longer afford to hand out lucrative contracts. Profits fell as government spending was cut back. Hard times lay ahead for industry.

Industrial disputes

To make matters worse, as far as the industrialists were concerned, the end of the war led to a wave of labour militancy. Wartime discipline in the factories, enforced by the military, was relaxed. Workers who had resented the longer hours, the fall in real wages caused by inflation and the ban on industrial action vented their frustration. During 1919 over a million workers took part in strikes and the membership of Socialist trade unions shot up from a quarter of a million in 1918 to two million in 1920.

Unemployment

Soldiers returning from the war were plunged into this deteriorating economic situation. The hoped-for prosperity was nowhere to be found. Industries whose profits were falling did not take on new workers. Unemployment was rising and broke the two million mark during 1919. To the soldiers this seemed a very poor reward for their sacrifices.

3 | The Socialist 'Threat'

As the economy worsened political divisions widened. The industrial workers flocked to the Socialist Party, whose membership rose from about 50,000 in 1914 to about 200,000 by 1919. The party had long abandoned the commitment to gradual reform that Giolitti had tried to encourage during the pre-war years. It now advocated revolution. Inspired by the Russian Revolution of 1917, Socialists called for the overthrow of the Liberal state. The goal, according to the party, was a 'Socialist republic' and the 'dictatorship of the **proletariat**' where private businesses and landed estates would be confiscated, and wealth shared. The 1919 congress made plain that to achieve this 'the proletariat must have recourse to the use of violence for the conquest of power over the **bourgeoisie**'.

Such extreme talk did not deter the voters. On the contrary, in the elections of November 1919, the first to be held under universal manhood suffrage, the Socialists swept through the northern cities, securing 32.4 per cent of the national vote and winning 156 seats. The party dedicated to revolution was now the largest single group in the Italian parliament.

Many middle class Italians were terrified. Their fears seemed confirmed when the new Socialist deputies interrupted the King's speech in parliament, shouting 'long live the Socialist republic', and then marched out singing the Socialist anthem, 'Red Flag' (*Bandiera Rossa*). Although this was empty posturing on the part of the Socialists – they had devoted no real thought to the question of how to bring about their revolution – many people feared that a '**Bolshevik**' seizure of power was imminent.

In this state of fear, many conservative Italians were disgusted that the government appeared to be doing nothing to meet the threat. Instead of using the power of the state to crush strikes and to harass Socialists, the Liberal government of Francesco Nitti was urging industrialists to make concessions to workers. Shopkeepers

Key question
Why were many middle class and conservative Italians terrified of Socialism, and unimpressed with the Liberal government's response to it?

Key date
Election made Socialists the single biggest party in the Italian parliament: November 1919

Key terms

Proletariat
Industrial working class.

Bourgeoisie
The middle classes, owners of businesses.

Bolshevik
Term for Communists.

had been alienated in June 1919, by what they saw as a government surrender to rioters who were protesting against the spiralling price of food. The government had set up food committees that had requisitioned supplies and set prices. The continuing inflation that had provoked the food riots was taken to be proof of government incompetence.

In addition, landowners were appalled by the government's failure to halt the spread of revolution to the countryside. Here many peasants were occupying uncultivated land and farming it for themselves. Agricultural labourers were joining Socialist trade unions in ever greater numbers, particularly in the province of Emilia Romagna, and were beginning to demand higher wages and guaranteed employment.

4 | 'Mutilated Victory'

Key question
Why did the peace settlement undermine support for the Liberal government?

It was not only over the issue of the supposed 'Socialist threat' that the right condemned the government. Nationalists, who had always considered the Liberals weak and incompetent at running the war, were now convinced that the government would fail to defend Italian interests at the peace conference. They demanded that Italy should not only receive those territories agreed with the Entente in 1915 (southern Tyrol, Trentino, Istria and parts of Dalmatia), but also be given the city of Fiume on the border of Istria (see the map on page 26). The Treaty of St Germain did cede Austrian land in the south Tyrol and the Trentino, but when Britain and the USA refused to hand over Fiume because the city was vital to the economy of the new Yugoslav state, the Nationalists blamed Liberal weakness. When, in addition, it became apparent that Italy would be denied Dalmatia because so few Italians lived there, and would not share in the division of German colonies in Africa, Nationalists were outraged. To them, Italy had been cheated. Her sacrifices had won only a '**mutilated victory**', and Liberalism was the culprit!

Key dates
Treaty of Versailles failed to award any German colonies to Italy: June 1919

Treaty of St Germain with Austria provided limited territorial gains for Italy: September 1919

Key term
Mutilated victory
The claim that Italy had been denied its rightful territorial gains in the peace settlement after the First World War.

Demobilised soldiers, struggling to adjust to civilian society and with work difficult to find, saw the peace settlement as a further humiliation. Many ex-officers, in particular, feared that the vibrant, expansionist Italy they had fought for was being undermined by a weak government. Their Italy was falling into the hands of Socialist revolutionaries who had opposed the war from the start and who had done their best to sabotage the war effort. For such men, Liberalism and the parliamentary system had proved abject failures. A powerful, dynamic Italy would have to be achieved by other methods.

Seizure of Fiume

Key question
Why did D'Annunzio's seizure of Fiume undermine the Liberal government?

In September 1919 the Nationalist intellectual Gabriele D'Annunzio led 2000 armed men into the city of Fiume and occupied it in defiance of the Italian government. Nationalists and many ex-soldiers hailed him as the embodiment of the Italy they wanted to create. D'Annunzio had shown that the way to achieve results was not to indulge in months of talking and negotiations, but rather to act decisively and not to be afraid to use force. Critics of the Liberal regime noted with satisfaction that the government lacked the will and the courage to use troops to end the occupation.

Seizure of Fiume by Nationalist Gabriele D'Annunzio: September 1919 — Key date

For over a year the flamboyant D'Annunzio ruled Fiume, drawing up fantastical constitutions for the city, while his armed supporters strutted through the streets. He became a public hero throughout Italy. His dramatic style, his eye for publicity and his high-volume denunciation of the government also made him something of a model for another enemy of Liberalism, Benito Mussolini. This ambitious journalist and politician, the leader of an insignificant political party when D'Annunzio marched into Fiume, was to become the first Fascist Prime Minister of Italy and, by 1925, would be the country's dictator.

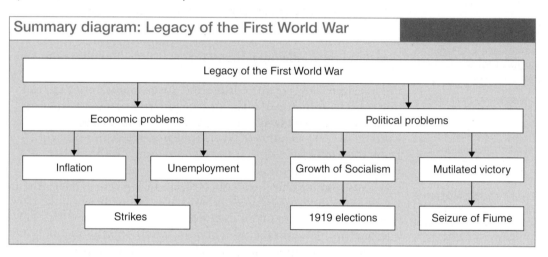

Summary diagram: Legacy of the First World War

- Legacy of the First World War
  - Economic problems
    - Inflation
    - Unemployment
    - Strikes
  - Political problems
    - Growth of Socialism
      - 1919 elections
    - Mutilated victory
      - Seizure of Fiume

5 | Mussolini and the Birth of Fascism

Key question
What were the ideas behind the early Fascist movement?

Benito Mussolini, the 36-year-old editor of *Il Popolo d'Italia*, shared D'Annunzio's contempt for Liberalism and hatred of Socialism. Although a former Socialist, the war had convinced him that Italy needed a regime that would end the struggle between social classes and, unlike the Liberals, provide dynamic leadership for Italy both at home and abroad. Mussolini himself might provide this new dynamic leadership together with the more energetic and patriotic of the former soldiers. From July 1918, he began to claim that *Il Popolo* was the 'newspaper of combatants and producers'. By producers he meant soldiers, farmers and factory workers. He tried to contrast these with those he regarded as the parasitic groups in Italian economy – businessmen who had made vast profits from wartime contracts, Socialists who had opposed the war and Liberal politicians.

Key dates

First meeting of Fascist movement: March 1919

Fascist failed to win any seats in election: November 1919

Key terms

Republicans
Wanted to abolish the monarchy.

Anarchists
Opposed both a strong central government and capitalism, arguing that political and economic power should be held by workers and peasants, organised at a local level.

Creation of the Fascist movement

By early 1919, Mussolini believed that it was time to translate his rhetoric into action. Accordingly, in March, he called the inaugural meeting of a new movement, the *Fasci di Combattimento*, or 'Combat Groups'. Only about 100 people came to Milan for the meeting. They represented a wide range of political views, including nationalists, **republicans**, **anarchists** and radical poets and painters. They had little in common except a hatred of the Liberal State and a contempt for the class struggle rhetoric of the Socialists. Nevertheless, they did manage to draw up a political programme that contained both demands for an expansionist Italy and the following, leftist, statements of intent:

1   A new National Assembly ... [will be set up].
2   Proclamation of the Italian Republic [abolition of the monarchy].

...

4   Abolition of all titles of nobility.

...

9   Suppression of all major companies, industrial or financial and of all speculation by banks and stock exchanges.
10   Control and taxation of private wealth. Confiscation of unproductive income (such as rent from the ownership of land or property).

...

12   Workers to have a significant share of the profits of the businesses they worked in.

Early failure

The early Fascist movement lacked the cohesion to form a disciplined political party. Indeed, when D'Annunzio occupied Fiume in late 1919, it was just another tiny grouping of radical agitators. What prominence Mussolini did have was due not to his self-proclaimed position as leader of Fascism, but rather to his aggressive journalism in *Il Popolo d'Italia*. The proof of his movement's failure seemed to come in the general election of November 1919. Not only did Mussolini himself fail to become a deputy, polling only 5000 out of the 270,000 votes cast in Milan, but Fascism performed dismally everywhere. Not a single seat was won in the new parliament and by the end of the year there were perhaps only 4000 declared Fascist supporters in the whole of Italy. The movement appeared doomed. However, Mussolini was to be saved by the government's inability to convince conservative Italians that it could deal with the supposed Socialist threat. From near oblivion in December 1919, the Fascists became, within the space of one year, a powerful force on the political scene.

Profile: Benito Mussolini 1883–1945

1883 – Born in Predappio, Romagna, the son of a devout Catholic schoolmistress and of a blacksmith with revolutionary views

1901 – Took job as elementary schoolteacher

1902 – Left for Switzerland where he lived in poverty, doing only odd-jobs

1904 – Returned to Italy, underwent military service

1906 – Journalist: his articles condemned the Church and advocated class struggle

1910 – Editor of a small Socialist newspaper paper in the town of Forli, in his home province

1911 – Jailed for attempting to stir up an insurrection against the war in Libya

1912 – Released from prison and appointed editor of *Avanti*, the Socialist party's newspaper

1914 – Resigned from *Avanti* and set up a new paper, *Il Popolo d'Italia* (The People of Italy). The paper claimed to be Socialist but it campaigned for Italian entry into the war

1915 – Married Rachele Guidi
– Conscripted into the army but only reached the rank of corporal

1917 – Invalided out of the army after an accident during a training exercise
– Took over editorship of *Il Popolo* once again. He blamed government defeatism and incompetence for the disaster of Caporetto, and claimed that Italy now needed a dictator who would direct the war effort with real energy

1919 – Founded the Fascist movement

Mussolini came from a humble background in a small town in central-northern Italy. He did not excel at school, being noted more for his overbearing manner and bullying nature than for his academic abilities. After a succession of minor teaching posts in village schools in which he showed little interest, and a brief period in Switzerland, Mussolini took up journalism. Taking up the cause of Socialism, his writing was aggressive and vitriolic. He condoned the use of violence and condemned the Liberal state and those reformist Socialists who wanted to co-operate with it. He made it plain that revolution was the only policy for the Socialist Party to pursue. Mussolini's journalism got him noticed and by 1912 he was editing the Socialists' own newspaper, *Avanti*.

The outbreak of the First World War was to alter Mussolini's career dramatically. His Socialist Party condemned the war as an imperialistic struggle fought at the expense of the working classes of Europe, and demanded that Italy remain neutral. But Mussolini saw the conflict as an event which would shake society to its foundations and bring revolution closer. Mussolini, now expelled from the Socialist Party, set up his own newspaper, *Il Popolo d'Italia*. Accepting financial support from companies such as Fiat, he campaigned vigorously in favour of intervention in the war.

Throughout 1918 his paper sought to create a new political movement which would promote both nationalism and social reform. He was trying to appeal to the soldiers who had no wish to return to rural and urban poverty once the war was over. Contemptuous of both Liberalism and Socialism, Mussolini founded the Fascist movement in March 1919.

Key question
Why did the Liberal government find it difficult to command majority support in the Italian parliament?

Key terms

Chamber of Deputies
The lower, but most important, house in the Italian parliament – similar to the British House of Commons

Anti-clericalism
Many Liberals were anti-clerical in the sense that they opposed the intrusion of the Catholic Church into politics. For example, they did not want Catholicism to be declared the official religion of Italy, and advocated civil rather than religious marriage ceremonies.

6 | The Rise of Fascism 1919–21

Liberal problems in parliament

The elections of November 1919 had disappointed Mussolini but had also caused great difficulties for the Liberal government. Liberals and their allies could muster only about 180 of the 508 seats and they still lacked cohesion and party discipline. The **Chamber of Deputies**, designed to protect and promote Liberalism, now contained a revolutionary Socialist Party holding 156 seats, and the Catholic Popular Party, the PPI, with 100 seats. The Liberal government led by the moderate Francesco Nitti did survive but it relied on support from Catholic deputies to maintain its fragile majority.

The PPI, or *Popolari* as it was known, had been founded in January 1919, when the Pope had finally lifted his ban on the formation of such a Catholic party. The *Popolari*, led by the Sicilian priest Don Sturzo, contained both conservative Catholics and Catholics determined to improve the lot of the peasantry. This was an uneasy coalition that found it easier to agree on what it opposed than what it stood for. It was reluctant to play a major role in government, but it was prepared to give its support to Liberal governments in return for concessions on policy. Despite this, the PPI remained deeply suspicious of Liberalism and did not forget the Liberals' traditional **anti-clericalism**.

Nitti's government was discredited by Fiume (see page 19) in the eyes of much of the public and was disliked by both the left and the right, for its unwillingness either to grant major reform or to crush protest. It struggled on until June 1920. But, with *Popolari* support waning, Nitti's fragile majority was unsustainable and he quietly resigned. He was replaced by the veteran Liberal Giovanni Giolitti. Once again the great exponent of *Trasformismo* (see page 7) attempted to appeal to both left and right – speaking of workers' entitlement to some say in management and at the same time planning to reduce the food subsidies that benefited the poor. Liberals, *Popolari* and even a handful of moderate Socialists joined his new coalition, but the majority Socialists were implacably hostile. Although he was an anti-clerical, the new Prime Minister still had to rely on Catholic support in the Chamber of Deputies to keep his government in power.

Socialist 'occupation of the factories'

Events outside parliament were to weaken Giolitti's government further. In September 1920 engineering workers, engaged in a dispute over wages, occupied their factories to prevent employers from locking them out. Within days, 400,000 workers from the northern cities were involved. The employers demanded that the government intervene to crush the occupation. However, Giolitti followed the policy of neutrality he had adopted in pre-war industrial disputes and stood aloof. He was convinced that the use of force would lead to a bloodbath, and believed that the occupation would soon collapse of its own accord. This policy enraged industrialists, particularly when the Prime Minister urged them to make concessions to the strikers. When it became apparent that a number of factories were being used to produce weapons for the strikers, conservatives feared that the revolution was now at hand. Again, in their eyes, the government was failing to do its duty. Even though the occupation was disorganised and collapsed within one month, as Giolitti had predicted, employers and conservatives did not forgive him for what they saw as his complacency and cowardice.

Socialist advances in the countryside

In the countryside, landowners were also complaining bitterly about a Socialist threat. Agricultural strikes and land occupations were continuing to increase. In Emilia, the Po Valley, Umbria and Tuscany (see map on page 26) Socialist trade unions were expanding and, with close to a million members, were beginning to establish a stranglehold over agricultural employment. In Emilia the unions demanded higher wages for agricultural labourers and guarantees that workers would not be laid off during quiet times of the year. Around Ferrara and Bologna a labourer could only gain employment through a job centre run by the Socialist Labourers' Union. If landowners resisted the trade unions' demands, their estates would face disruption and their farm managers might be subject to physical attack.

The power of the Socialists was shown not only in agricultural disputes but also in local elections, held in late 1920. The Socialists found themselves in control of 26 of the country's 69 provinces, mainly those located in north and central Italy. The Socialist party was particularly strong in Emilia where it controlled 80 per cent of the local councils. The urban middle classes feared that the Socialists would now raise local taxes on the better-off. Shopkeepers were concerned about the potential competition from the spread of Socialist-sponsored co-operative shops. These shops were designed to offer cheap prices to customers and, at the same time, to allow the shopworkers a say in the running of the business and a share of the profits.

Key question
How did the actions of the Liberal government alienate many conservative Italians and big business?

Key date

Occupation of the factories by 400,000 engineering workers: September 1920

Key question
Why did Fascism attract growing support in the countryside of central and northern Italy?

Key date

Start of Fascist squad violence: November 1920

Anti-Socialist backlash

Landowners and conservatives felt themselves an embattled class. Their political enemies and social inferiors seemed to be in the ascendancy and they thought they had been abandoned by the government. This sense of abandonment was intensified by the government's decision to allow agricultural labourers to keep the unused land they had illegally occupied.

By the end of 1920 the right-wingers in the provinces of northern and central Italy began to fight back. Desperate measures, including the use of violence, appeared justified in the face of revolution. In Emilia and Tuscany, in particular, frightened landowners and middle class townsfolk began to turn to local Fascist groups who shared their hatred of Socialism and needed little encouragement to attack Socialists. November 1920 saw one of the first examples of Fascist violence when the inauguration of the new Socialist council in Bologna turned into a riot. These Fascist squads were often small and lacking in any coherent ideology, but they proved adept at burning down Socialist offices and beating up trade unionists. Their enemies might also find themselves being forced to drink litres of potentially lethal castor oil, a punishment that quickly became a trademark for Fascist thugs.

The violence continued through the winter and spring of 1921, destroying over 80 trade union offices and leaving 200 dead and 800 wounded. By spring, Emilia and Tuscany had become strongholds of the Fascist squads. The police had looked the other way as *squadrismo* had crushed the Socialist power in these provinces.

Key term

Squadrismo
The violent attacks of Fascist gangs, or squads.

A carefully staged photo of blackshirted Fascist squads. Look carefully at the photograph: what message is it trying to convey about *squadrismo*?

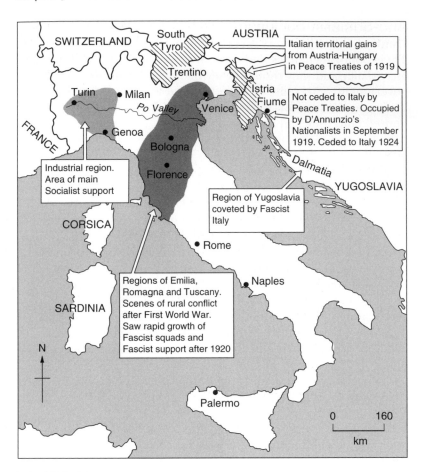

Italy 1918–25.

The map shows the following labels:

SWITZERLAND • AUSTRIA • South Tyrol • Trentino • Turin • Milan • Po Valley • Venice • Istria • Fiume • Genoa • Bologna • Florence • Dalmatia • YUGOSLAVIA • CORSICA • Rome • SARDINIA • Naples • Palermo • FRANCE • N

Italian territorial gains from Austria-Hungary in Peace Treaties of 1919

Not ceded to Italy by Peace Treaties. Occupied by D'Annunzio's Nationalists in September 1919. Ceded to Italy 1924

Industrial region. Area of main Socialist support

Region of Yugoslavia coveted by Fascist Italy

Regions of Emilia, Romagna and Tuscany. Scenes of rural conflict after First World War. Saw rapid growth of Fascist squads and Fascist support after 1920

0   160
km

Fascist supporters

In their early days the Fascist squads consisted mainly of middle class students and demobilised soldiers, usually ex-army officers and more junior ranks, such as sergeants and corporals. But, as they proved their ability to intimidate the Socialists, the squads began to attract new followers. Many of the recruits were small farmers, farm managers and sharecroppers who, although far from rich, comprised the better-off peasantry. They were likely to be ambitious and anxious to buy their own land. Socialist talk of higher wage rates and **collectivisation** of land angered them.

At the end of 1921 Fascism had probably a little over 200,000 active supporters. Roughly 50 per cent were ex-servicemen, but there were also landowners, shopkeepers, clerical workers and even teachers. There were workers in the squads but the leadership was overwhelmingly middle class. It was also apparent that Fascism was a movement that attracted the young: almost 10 per cent of members were students and 25 per cent were below voting age. For such people the Fascists seemed an exciting contrast to the staid old men of Liberal politics.

Among the older generation, many people who had previously supported the conservative wing of Liberalism now despaired of the seemingly ineffectual parliamentary system and saw Fascism

Key question
What types of people were attracted to Fascism and why?

Collectivisation
Seizure of private land by the state. The land would then be re-organised into state-run farms or distributed to groups of peasants.

Key term

as a way of securing the disciplined state for which they longed. However, it would be wrong to conclude that Fascism was hijacked by conservatives. The Fascist leaders in the provinces still thought of themselves as leading a revolutionary movement that would overthrow the state by force in a *coup d'état*. Men like Roberto Farinacci, Italo Balbo and Dino Grandi remained dedicated to violent *squadrismo*.

Profile: Italo Balbo 1896–1940

1896	–	Born in Quartesana, Italy
1915–18	–	War service. Awarded medals for bravery and reached rank of captain
1919–20	–	University student and bank worker
1921	–	Leader of Fascist squads in Ferrara, in central Italy. In September, he led a march of 3000 Fascists against Socialists in Ravenna
1922	–	Led Fascist squads in a rampage across the province of the Romagna, noting in his diary: 'It was a night of terror. Our passage was signed by plumes of smoke and fire' Demanded that Mussolini march on Rome to seize power
1923	–	Implicated in murder of anti-Fascist Catholic priest
1924	–	Appointed Commander of Fascist militia
1926	–	Appointed Secretary of State for Air and expanded Italian airforce
1929		Appointed minister of the airforce
1930	–	Led flight of 12 flying boats in one of first trans-Atlantic crossings from Italy to Brazil
1933	–	Led flight of 24 flying boats from Rome to Chicago, USA
	–	Appointed governor-general of Libya
1940	–	Shot down and killed when his plane was hit by Italian anti-aircraft fire over Libya

Balbo was in many ways a typical Fascist *Ras*. An ex-serviceman with a taste for violence and a hatred of Socialism, he built up his powerbase in the area around Ferrara in central Italy. He was one of a number of prominent Fascists who pressurised Mussolini into action in October 1922, demanding that he seize power by force if necessary.

With the Fascist dictatorship established from 1926, Balbo used his ministerial post to build up the prestige of Fascism abroad through his highly publicised trans-Atlantic flights. Balbo's own high profile may have caused Mussolini to see him as a potential rival: it has been suggested that his appointment as the governor of Libya was Mussolini's ploy to get Balbo out of Italy and out of the public eye. Indeed, Balbo's widow believed that his death in 1940 was no accident, rather an assassination on Mussolini's orders.

Profile: Roberto Farinacci 1892–1945

1892	– Born in Isernia, Italy
1909	– Railway worker in Cremona. Attracted by Socialism
1914–15	– Campaigned for Italy's entry into the First World War
1915–18	– Enlisted as soldier but called back from the front as skilled railway workers were needed for the war effort. Began to write for *Il Popolo d'Italia*
1919	– Attended first meeting of Fascist movement
	– Organised Fascist squads in Cremona
1920–1	– As *Ras* of Fascist squads in Cremona he attacked Socialists and their trade unions, and terrorised the local populace
	– Physically attacked an opposition MP in the Chamber of Deputies
1922	– Appointed himself Mayor of Cremona
	– Pressed Mussolini to March on Rome
1925	– Appointed Fascist Party Secretary
1926	– Dismissed as Party Secretary
1935	– General in the Fascist militia during war against Ethiopia
	– Appointed to Fascist Grand Council
1938	– Advocate of anti-Semitic policies
1943–5	– Supporter of Mussolini's 'Italian Social Republic' – puppet regime under effective Nazi control
1945	– Executed by Italian anti-Fascists

Farinacci's early career had similarities to that of Mussolini. Both came from humble backgrounds and were active Socialists. The First World War made them reject this Socialism and convinced them that Italy needed a new, radical political movement that would sweep away Liberalism. Farinacci was one of Mussolini's earliest supporters, and his squads in Cremona were among the most violent in Italy.

After Mussolini became Prime Minister, Farinacci pressed for the establishment of a dictatorship and continued use of violence against opponents. Appointed party secretary in 1925, his clamour for more radical policies contributed to his dismissal the following year. Although he no longer held a national position, Farinacci maintained great power over Cremona.

Returning to national prominence in the late 1930s he became pro-Nazi, advocating both **anti-Semitism** and Italy's entry into the Second World War.

Anti-Semitism
Hatred of Jews.

Key term

Mussolini's control over Fascist *squadrismo*

Local Fascist leaders, such as the young and aggressive ex-army officer Italo Balbo in Ferrara and the equally callous Dino Grandi in Bologna, built up their own power. Mussolini had not been the guiding hand behind the Fascist violence, but he soon saw the political opportunities *squadrismo* offered. He strove to put himself

Key question
How did Mussolini gain control over local Fascist squads?

at the forefront of this *squadrismo* by reasserting his claim to be the sole and undisputed leader of the movement. There was reluctance on the part of the *Ras* to surrender their independence, but Mussolini seems to have been able to convince even the most ambitious of them that their success depended on his leadership. His was the dominant personality in the Fascist movement and his newspaper could publicise Fascist activities. He argued that, without his leadership, Fascism would lack all coherence as the various factions would fall out among themselves. With Mussolini as leader, Fascism could be presented as a national movement with a vision of a new Italy. Mussolini, the journalist, could depict Fascist violence not as simple thuggery, but rather as a painful necessity if Italy was to be saved from Bolshevism. *Squadrismo* would be viewed as an anti-Socialist crusade. In his speech to the Fascists of Bologna in April 1921 Mussolini tried to create this crusading image.

> However much violence may be deplored, it is evident that we, in order to make our ideas understood, must beat refractory skulls with resounding blows … But … we are violent [only] because it is necessary to be so.
>
> Our punitive expeditions, all those acts of violence which figure in the papers, must always have the character of the just retort and legitimate reprisal; because we are the first to recognise that it is sad, after having fought the external enemy [in the First World War], to have to fight the enemy within … The Socialists had formed a State within a State … [and] this State is more tyrannical, illiberal and overbearing than the old one, [so the violence] … which we are causing today is a revolution to break up the Bolshevist State.

Electoral breakthrough: May 1921

Key question
Why were the Fascists able to win seats in parliament?

Key date
Fascists gained 35 seats in election for Italian parliament: May 1921

While thus justifying and encouraging violent *squadrismo*, Mussolini was also careful to suggest to Liberal politicians that all this talk of violence and revolution might be little more than bluster. Giolitti was taken in – he claimed the Fascists were just 'fireworks: they'll make a great deal of noise but only leave smoke behind'. Giolitti saw Fascism as just another political force that could be absorbed into the Liberal system. Mussolini did his best to encourage this belief. Persuaded that the self-styled leader of Fascism was more an opportunist than an extremist, Giolitti offered an electoral alliance that he hoped would produce an anti-Socialist governing coalition.

Fascists and Giolittian Liberals co-operated during the general election held in May 1921. But despite this new air of respectability, the Fascist squads continued their work, killing about 100 Socialist sympathisers during the election campaign. Again, the police tended to turn a blind eye – this was what the 'Bolshevists' deserved! However, the election results proved that the violence and intimidation had not deterred the voters. The Socialists remained the largest party in the Chamber, holding 123 seats, followed by the *Popolari* with 107. If Giolitti was disappointed that the Socialist vote had held up, Mussolini was satisfied with the progress that his party had made. The Fascists had secured seven per cent of the total vote and had won 35 seats. Mussolini was now a deputy.

Mussolini speaking in the Colosseum, Rome, in 1920. The photograph gives an indication of Mussolini's forceful oratory style. Note too the stress on military-style uniforms. The choice of venue was designed to associate Fascism with the glories of Ancient Rome.

Summary diagram: Rise of Fascism 1919–21

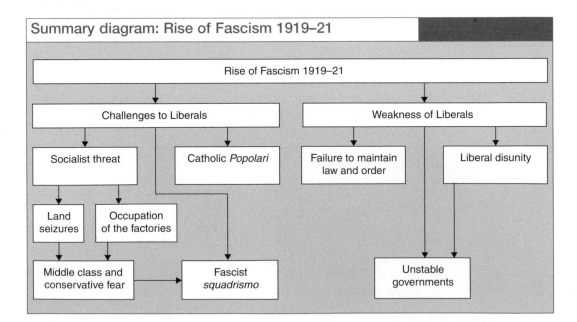

Key question
What tactics did
Mussolini use to
generate support
from conservative
groups and from
Liberal politicians?

7 | Mussolini Seizes the Initiative: May 1921–October 1922

The elections had given Mussolini what he wanted: an air of respectability and a foothold in parliament. He had no wish to be absorbed into Liberalism, to be a junior partner in a coalition, as Giolitti had intended. Consequently, he announced that the Fascists would not, after all, support Giolitti's government.

Mussolini now saw the possibility of achieving real power. He had no master-plan but he was an extremely astute politician. He knew that he needed to demonstrate to the Italian public, to industrialists, landowners and the middle classes in particular, that Liberalism was finished as a political movement. Unstable, short-lived governments unable to maintain law and order or deal with the country's economic problems would provide proof of this. He also had to convince these crucial groups in society that only Fascism could stop the Socialists and restore order and discipline to Italian society. Furthermore, he realised that for Fascism to become acceptable to the middle classes and conservatives it must either abandon or play down any remaining ideas about radical economic and social reform. During 1921 and 1922 Mussolini skilfully took advantage of his opportunities to create such an impression.

Government instability

Governments following the elections of May 1921 were unstable. Giolitti did manage to form a coalition without Mussolini but it collapsed within a month. The *Popolari* had withdrawn its support when Giolitti proposed to introduce a tax which would have had the side-effect of hitting the Vatican's financial investments. Without the tacit support of this Catholic Party, with its 107 deputies in parliament, it was now virtually impossible for any government to survive, yet the *Popolari* were suspicious of the anti clerical traditions of Liberalism and was willing to destroy any government that offended it.

To make matters worse, the Liberals were divided among themselves. Liberalism was still plagued by factions centred on prominent politicians, notably Giolitti, Salandra, Facta and Orlando, and these leaders actively disliked one another. In such circumstances it was not surprising that the three Italian governments between May 1921 and October 1922 were fragile and unable to introduce the decisive measures needed to cope with the industrial disruption and the collapse of law and order.

Collapse of law and order

The progressive collapse of law and order owed a great deal to Fascist actions. *Squadrismo* continued through 1921. Socialists were attacked, and not infrequently killed. Fascist violence even extended to parliament itself, most notoriously on the occasion when a Socialist deputy was beaten up on the floor of the chamber.

Mussolini increases his control over the Fascist movement

Mussolini's activities during the remainder of 1921 were directed towards making Fascism a cohesive political force that could command more widespread support within Italian society. His attempt to organise Fascism more effectively resulted in the establishment of the **National Fascist Party** in October 1921. Fascism was no longer just a movement, but a recognised political party. In the following month the party congress formally accepted Mussolini as the leader of Fascism. The party was to be organised and run by men from Mussolini's own Milan faction, who were loyal to their leader. Mussolini had established more control over those Fascist squads that had so terrorised Socialists in the agricultural areas of Emilia and the Romagna. However, his control over this provincial Fascism was by no means total, and there would be disagreements over the means to secure power. Yet he could now pose as the unchallenged head of a real political party.

Key date

National Fascist Party organisation created: October 1921

Reassuring the Catholic Church and conservative Italians

In November 1921 Mussolini made a direct attempt to win over Catholics. He declared Fascism to be opposed to divorce, in agreement with the *Popolari*, that the peasants deserved a better deal, and he prepared to settle the **Roman question** on terms acceptable to the Pope.

Mussolini also increased his efforts to appeal to conservatives – people who feared Socialism, deplored the government's conciliatory policy towards labour, and questioned its ability to restore order. He dropped the left-wing policies espoused by Fascism in 1919. In fact, the leader of Fascism had begun to distance himself from such radical ideas during 1920, and it had not been coincidental that the 35 Fascist deputies elected in May 1921 were on the right of the movement. From 1921 Mussolini's speeches concentrated on what Fascism was against, namely Socialism and Liberalism, but spelled out Fascist policies only in very broad terms, stressing its patriotism and commitment to strong government. A good example of this approach is the speech he gave in September 1922 in the city of Udine.

Key terms

National Fascist Party
Set up by Mussolini to unite the Fascist movement and to increase his control over local Fascist squads and their leaders.

Roman question
The question of the role of the Catholic Church in the Italian state, including the territorial claims of the Pope over Rome, the issues of civil and church marriage and divorce.

Our programme is simple: we wish to govern Italy.
We must have a State which will simply say: 'The State does not represent a party, it represents the nation as a whole, it includes all, is over all, protects all.'
This is the State that must arise from the Italy of Vittorio Veneto. A State ... which is not like the Liberal State ... a State which does not fall under the power of the Socialists. ...
We [also] want to remove from the State all its economic attributes. We have had enough of the State railwayman, the State postman and the State insurance official. We have had enough of the State administration at the expense of Italian taxpayers, which has done nothing but aggravate the exhausted financial condition

of the country. [The new state will] still control the police, who protect honest men from the attacks of thieves ... [and] the army that must guarantee the inviolability of the country and foreign policy.

Such speeches were quite deliberate attempts to persuade the conservative classes that they had nothing to fear and much to gain from the victory of Fascism. They also reflected Fascism's lack of specific, detailed policies. Mussolini wanted a strong, expansionist Italy, hated Socialism and democracy, and despised parliament, but he was principally concerned with winning power for himself and becoming dictator of Italy. Policy was completely subordinated to this end. In fact, it was advantageous to have little clear policy – no groups would be offended.

Fascist violence

Key question
How did Mussolini make use of Fascist violence to help his rise to power?

Mussolini was concerned that the increasing Fascist violence, even if directed at Socialists, might go too far and provoke conservatives to demand that the authorities crush the Fascists and restore law and order. This was a real danger and it was clear to Mussolini that the police and army had the power to destroy his movement. That he managed to calm conservatives, yet avoid splits within his party was proof of his political skills. On the one hand he encouraged the squads to continue their campaign of violence and suggested that he agreed with their plans for a violent seizure of power. On the other hand, when talking to conservatives, he disassociated himself from the worst excesses of Fascist violence. He would suggest that the perpetrators were responsible whom he would discipline, but would also imply that only he could curb these excesses. If conservatives wanted to avoid a violent conflict with Fascism they should come to an accommodation with him. If they conceded some share of political power to Fascism, he would ensure that Fascism became a more respectable party.

This dual policy was followed throughout 1922. In the spring Fascist squads rampaged through north-central Italy attacking Socialist town councils and trade union property. In May the town council of Bologna was actually driven out of office. During July street-fighting took place in most of the northern cities. During this time Mussolini talked to the various Liberal factions, stressing Fascist power but also suggesting that he was far from being a rabid revolutionary. He implied that he was interested in a parliamentary alliance that would bring the Fascists into government. In such circumstances the fragile government coalition lacked the political will to use the police to curb the violence of a party that might soon be joining them in office. In any case, the police were reluctant to intervene in the street-fighting – they had no love for the Socialists and in some areas they had even loaned weapons to the local Fascist squads.

The general strike

At the end of July the Socialist trade unions called a general strike in an attempt to force the government to act against the Fascists. Mussolini made brilliant use of this opportunity to demonstrate that the left was still a threat and that only Fascism could deal with it. As soon as the general strike was announced, he publicly declared that if the government did not stop the industrial action his Fascists would step in and do it for them. Almost as the strike began, Fascists took over the running of public transport and ensured that the postal system continued to function. If strikers protested they were beaten up.

The general strike proved a fiasco for the left. It had been poorly organised, and only attracted partial support from the workers. Even in those cities where the strike call was obeyed, the Fascist action limited its effect. Within days the strike had collapsed, leaving the Socialists in disarray. Mussolini could present his Fascists as the sole defenders of law and order. This was a crucial development. The Fascists' actions impressed the conservative middle classes, helping to convince them that Fascism could be trusted with a share in government. From this point on the question was not whether the Fascists would enter the government, but rather on what terms.

Key date

Socialist general strike: July 1922

8 | The March on Rome

Mussolini launched himself into further negotiations with the Liberal factions, discussing which cabinet posts should be allocated to the Fascists. He did not disclose that his real ambition was to be Prime Minister. At the same time he was talking to the Fascist squads about organising a *coup d'état*. In fact, he was under great pressure to adopt such a policy – many Fascists had wanted to try to seize power at the end of the abortive general strike and it had taken all of Mussolini's authority to dissuade them. He believed that he could achieve power without a coup, but by considering such action he could keep his more radical supporters happy, and intimidate the Liberals into making concessions. At the beginning of October Mussolini increased the pressure by starting to organise a Fascist march on Rome.

The Fascist squads were organised into a militia and plans were drawn up to seize the major towns and cities of northern and central Italy. Around 30,000 Fascists would then converge on the capital and install themselves in power. If they met resistance they would crush it. Many Fascists genuinely believed that their coup was finally at hand. However, their leader saw the march as his ultimate piece of political blackmail. Mussolini seems to have been convinced that, under such a threat, the politicians would agree that he should become Prime Minister.

While going ahead with preparations for the march, Mussolini took care to reassure the establishment that they need not fear a Fascist government. In particular, he stressed that Fascism and the monarchy could work together, as the following speech, which he made at Naples on the eve of the march, makes clear.

Key question
Why was Mussolini appointed Prime Minister?

Mussolini with Fascist *Ras*. What impression is the photograph intended to convey about the Fascist Party and Mussolini's position within it?

Fascists seized key buildings in northern cities, in preparation for the march on Rome: 27 October 1922

Resignation of last Liberal government: 28 October 1922

Mussolini invited to become Prime Minister: 29 October 1922

There is no doubt that the unity of Italy is soundly based on the House of Savoy [the royal family]. There is equally no doubt that the Italian monarchy cannot put itself in opposition to the new national forces. It did not manifest any opposition when the Italian people asked and obtained their country's participation in the war. Would it then have reason to be in opposition today, when *Fascismo* does not intend to attack the regime, but rather to free it from all those superstructures that overshadow its historical position and limit the expansion of the national spirit?

The parliament and all the paraphernalia of democracy have nothing in common with the monarchy. Not only this, but neither do we want to take away the people's toy – the parliament. We say 'toy' because a great part of the people seem to see it this way. Can you tell me else why, out of 11 million voters, six million do not trouble themselves to vote? But we will not take it away.

Mussolini realised that the attitude of the King was critical. As commander-in-chief he could order the army to crush Fascism if he so wished.

By the last week of October preparations were complete. On the night of the 27th, Fascist squads seized town halls, telephone exchanges and railway stations throughout northern Italy. In the early hours of 28 October the government of Luigi Facta finally found the courage to act, and persuaded the King to agree to the declaration of a state of siege. Police and troops prepared to disperse the Fascist gangs converging on Rome by road and rail. However, by 9 am King Victor Emmanuel had changed his mind. He now refused to authorise the declaration of martial law that would have sanctioned the use of force against the Fascists. This would prove to be a fateful decision: it was a sign that the King lacked confidence in his government and was anxious to avoid a violent showdown with Mussolini's Fascists.

It is still uncertain why Victor Emmanuel made this decision – he may have over-estimated the number of Fascists marching on Rome and feared a civil war; he may have feared that his cousin, the Duke of Aosta, a known Fascist sympathiser, was waiting to depose him if he acted against Mussolini. Probably more plausibly, the King had little love for the existing Liberal politicians and, believing Mussolini's protestations of loyalty, considered that Fascists should be brought into the governing coalition. Their nationalism, their anti-Socialism and their energy might breathe new life into the regime. Victor Emmanuel certainly did not realise that his decision would open the way for a Fascist dictatorship.

On hearing of the King's refusal to declare martial law, Facta's government resigned. Victor Emmanuel then approached Salandra, a veteran conservative Liberal, and asked him to form a new government. Salandra attempted to negotiate with the Fascists, offering them a few cabinet posts, but it soon became apparent that Mussolini would accept nothing less than the post of Prime Minister for himself. With other Liberal leaders also opposed to a Salandra premiership – a sign of the continuing faction-fighting – the King realised that he needed to find a different man to head the government. In the apparent absence of any other viable candidate Benito Mussolini was asked, on 29 October, to become Prime Minister of Italy.

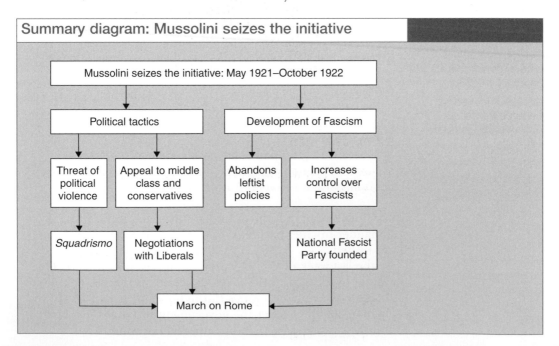

Summary diagram: Mussolini seizes the initiative

Mussolini poses in the formal attire of a conventional Italian politician.

9 | Key Debate

To what extent was Mussolini's success the result of Liberal weakness?

In the 1930s the exiled Italian intellectual G.A. Borgese reflected:

> She [Italy] was the last born among the nations [of western Europe].
>   There was no reason for, and no possibility of making Italy the centre of the universe ... But she might have been a beacon for all, a thing of beauty.
>   Why did it not happen?

Why was [Liberal] Italy so short-lived?

A course of about 50 years is less than what is ordinarily granted to the natural development of an individual life. That nation, the Italy of the *Risorgimento*, did not exceed by much the duration of half a century.

In 1922 Fascism came.

The question of why Fascism came to Italy has generated great historical debate. The fact that Fascism emerged first in Italy, pre-dating Hitler's Nazi regime by over 10 years, has directed further attention towards the issue.

An aberration?

To Renzo de Felice, the most prominent Italian historian on the period, Fascism was something of an aberration, an unfortunate episode separating Liberal Italy from the democratic Italy of post-1945. The **Liberal historian** Benedetto Croce, writing in the 1930s and 1940s, was one of the first to describe Fascism as a 'momentary contagion'. For him and his fellow Liberals, the rise of Fascism had nothing to do with any failings of the Liberal regime, but was the was the result of the shock of the First World War and the Russian revolution, with their dire social and economic consequences. To such writers, the pre-Fascist regime had represented something of a 'beacon for all', in Borgese's words.

Failure of the state

To those on the left this was sentimental nonsense. For them, Fascism was the result of the utter failure of the new Italian state. The Liberal regime had been foisted on the Italian people, made no attempt to represent or involve the masses in political life, and far from upholding political liberties, willingly employed repression against popular protest. Politics was the preserve of a wealthy élite dedicated not to the public good, but rather to the pursuit of personal power and financial gain.

This interpretation was summed up by the **Marxist historian** Antonio Gramsci, writing in the 1930s.

> The leaders of the *Risorgimento* said they were aiming at the creation of a modern state in Italy, and they in fact produced a bastard. They aimed at stimulating the formation of an extensive and energetic ruling class and they did not succeed, at integrating the people into the framework of the new state, and they did not succeed. The paltry political life …, the fundamental rebelliousness of the Italian popular classes, the narrow existence of a cowardly ruling stratum, they are all consequences of that failure.

Few modern historians would go so far in their condemnation of the Liberal regime, but most would agree that the Italian political system was unstable on the eve of the First World War, and that the war only worsened the problems.

Key terms

Liberal historian
A historian who sympathises with the Liberal regime, arguing that Italy, prior to Fascism, was maturing into a stable, parliamentary democracy.

Marxist historian
A historian who broadly subscribes to the views of Karl Marx. Argues that Liberal regimes are a guise for the exploitation of the working class and that such regimes will be overthrown once the working class realise and exert their political strength.

Fear of Socialism

Alexander De Grand, a leading US historian, has argued that the First World War worsened class conflict, and that Fascism grew out of the reaction to the rapid rise of Socialism. When the Socialists became the largest political party in parliament in 1919, the rich and the middle classes were terrified. As Liberal governments appeared to have little answer to the Socialist strikes and land seizures, Italians with more conservative views began to look for a more dynamic response that would restore law and order and protect their interests. This response took the form of anti-Socialist violence in the towns and countryside of central-northern Italy. De Grand stresses the importance of these violent Fascist squads in generating new recruits for Fascism and in establishing the credibility of the Fascist movement.

Role of Mussolini

Denis Mack Smith, the most prominent British writer on modern Italian history, accepts the importance of violent *squadrismo*, but emphasises the key role of Mussolini in making political capital out of this disorder. For example, his *Popolo d'Italia* took every opportunity to exaggerate the Socialist threat and to depict Fascists not as violent thugs, but as selfless individuals devoted to creating their vision of Italy, an Italy of peace and stability, an Italy of social harmony, an Italy respected in the world. This image proved attractive to many Italians.

Mussolini's astute political skills were seen in his realisation that the route to power lay through winning conservative support. Consequently, he abandoned the radical programme set out in 1919 and took care to appear as a moderate when talking to Liberals. He avoided committing himself to any clear policy programme and altered his message according to the audience he was addressing. Mussolini would speak to Fascists of his determination to transform Italian society radically, yet tell Liberals that his real goal was simply to destroy Socialism and to inject some energy into the political system. Mussolini's ability to reassure Liberals proved vital in securing his appointment as Prime Minister in October 1922.

Liberal failings

Mack Smith does not accept the argument of Marxist historians, such as Gramsci, that the rise of Fascism was simply the deliberate attempt of Liberals, and their conservative and big business allies, to crush the growing power of the Italian working class. For him, Liberalism after 1918 was characterised by weakness and division. The arrival of mass democracy meant that parliament was no longer dominated by Liberals, yet the Liberal leaders tried to maintain the old style of politics. There was still no coherent Liberal party. There was just a series of factions based around prominent personalities. The Liberal governments of the post-war years were, in consequence, particularly fragile coalitions unable and often unwilling either to grant reform or to direct the forces of the state (the police and the army) to uphold the law. Governments lost control of events and politics began to take to the streets.

Liberal failings were compounded by the uncooperative attitude of the Catholics. A parliamentary alliance between Liberals and the *Popolari* to form a government of the centre-right might well have reassured conservatives and made the growth of Fascism more difficult. Giolitti did try to form a working alliance in 1921, but mutual mistrust ensured that the alliance was short lived.

Unable to form stable coalitions, fearful of the Socialist threat, and unsure of how to respond to the growing disorder, many Liberals allowed themselves to be convinced that only a Fascist presence in government could crush the Socialists, revitalise parliament as an institution and restore confidence in the regime. Thus, when Mussolini was appointed Prime Minister in October 1922 they were not dismayed: in their naivety they believed that Mussolini could be transformed into a 'normal' politician.

Some key books in the debate

R.J.B. Bosworth, *The Italian Dictatorship: Problems and Perspectives in the Interpretation of Mussolini and Fascism* (Arnold, 1998).

A.J. De Grand, *Italian Fascism – Its Origins and Development* (University of Nebraska, 2000).

N. Farrell, *Mussolini: A New Life* (Weidenfeld, 2003).

Denis Mack Smith, *Mussolini* (Granada, 1983).

Study Guide: AS Questions

In the style of AQA

Course essay: Examine the extent to which political instability in Italy in the years 1918 to 1920 was the result of Italian involvement in the First World War.

Source: AQA, January 2006

Study tips

The cross-references are intended to take you straight to the material that will help you to answer the question.

The course essay gives you the opportunity to prepare a detailed plan on no more than two sides of A4. You will have this plan in front of you in the examination hall when you come to write the course essay.

Before you write your detailed plan, you will need to identify examples of political instability 1918–20. These should include:

- The challenge to Liberal dominance in parliament from the Socialists and *Popolari* (page 23).
- The beginnings of the Fascist challenge to Liberalism.
- The inability to form lasting coalition governments (page 31).

- Signs of political arguments and instability in the streets and countryside of Italy, notably in the form of strikes, land seizures, and the very beginnings of Fascist violence (pages 24–9).
- The challenge to the government posed by the invasion of Fiume (pages 19–20).

Once you have done this, you need to consider why this instability occurred. The following table should help you organise your thoughts:

Example of political instability 1918–20	Ways in which First World War helped cause this instability	Other causes of this instability
Challenge from Socialism and *Popolari*		
Beginnings of Fascist challenge		
Weak coalition governments		
Strikes, land seizures, violence		
Fiume		

This table will help you to decide the extent to which Italian involvement in the First World War led to political instability, so you can now start on your detailed plan.

You might decide to begin your essay with a discussion of what political instability was caused principally by the First World War before moving on to examples where the war was less significant.

To achieve a high mark it is vital to explain how causes link together. For example, wartime inflation and poor working conditions led to growing support for the Socialists who not only challenged the Liberals in parliament, but also encouraged strikes. Ensure that your plan will enable you to explain these links.

Finally remember to:

- Check that every paragraph directly refers back to the question
- Stick to the word limit.
- Check that your conclusion contains a reasoned judgement on the overall significance of the First World War in causing political instability.

In the style of Edexcel

(a) In what ways did the economic difficulties experienced by Italians lead to political problems within Italy immediately after the First World War? (20 marks)

(b) Why was there a crisis in government by 1922? (40 marks)

Exam tips

The cross-references are intended to take you straight to the material that will help you to answer the questions.

(a) You will have roughly 15 minutes in the exam to write your answer and should aim to explain both the nature of the economic problems and, crucially, how each one had political consequences. Your answer should include:
- Inflation – its impact on different groups of Italians and the political reactions to it (page 17).
- Industrial strikes – causes and consequences (pages 18 and 24).
- Land seizures – the growth of Socialist activity and the emergence of Fascist squads (page 24).

Do point out the links between these factors. For example, inflation fuelled labour militancy, leading to strikes and the growth of support for Socialism. The growth of Socialism terrified many middle class Italians, leading to Fascist violence against Socialists.

(b) It is vital that you do not write an account of the events in Italy from 1919 to 1922. Such a narrative approach will attain less than half marks. Instead, you should identify those factors that helped to cause a crisis in Italy. These factors should include:
- Growth of Socialism (pages 18–19).
- Fascist *squadrismo* and the breakdown of law and order (pages 24–35).
- The difficulties in forming and sustaining Liberal governments (pages 31–6).
- Mussolini's actions (pages 20–40).

Do remember that each factor will require factual examples. For example, you should give examples of where Fascist *squadrismo* took place and how many people were killed (page 25). But it is also important to give a detailed explanation of the implications of this for the weakening of government authority. In this way, you will be linking this factor to the question.

When writing your answer it is very important that you link these factors together to show how accumulating difficulties led to a crisis. For example, you should explain how the growth of Socialism undermined the credibility of Liberal governments and led to the emergence of the Fascist squads. Finally, your last paragraph should sum up the key elements of the crisis of October 1922: different Liberal leaders negotiating with Mussolini to bring the Fascists into a new government and the threat of a march on Rome.

You should spend approximately 35 minutes on part (b).

In the style of OCR

How far do you agree that popular dissatisfaction with Italian governments after the First World War was the main reason for Mussolini's rise to power? (45 marks)

Source: OCR, June 2003

Exam tips

The cross-references are intended to take you straight to the material that will help you to answer the question.

It is essential that you focus on the key phrase in the question 'popular dissatisfaction' with Liberal governments. You must consider which groups of Italians were dissatisfied with the Liberals and why. You should include:

- Why many working class Italians were attracted to Socialism and disliked the Liberals (pages 17–18).
- Why many middle class and conservative Italians saw Liberal governments as weak and ineffective (pages 18–19).

You should now identify and explain those other factors that contributed to Mussolini's rise to power. For example:

- Balance of parties in parliament which led to unstable governments (page 23).
- Fear of Socialism leading to Fascist *squadrismo* (pages 24–5).
- Mussolini's actions (pages 20–40).

To achieve high marks you must show how these factors linked together to help the rise of Fascism. For example, the growth of Socialism terrified the middle classes and led to the emergence of the Fascist squads. Lastly, you must make a judgement and justify it: was popular dissatisfaction with the Liberals the main cause of Fascism's rise or were other factors, such as the tactics of Mussolini, more important?

4 Mussolini: From Prime Minister to Dictator 1922–8

POINTS TO CONSIDER

Mussolini became Prime Minister in October 1922, but was still far from being the 'all-powerful' dictator of Italy. Over the next six years he would:

- Increase his power over government, parliament and the Fascist movement
- Reform election law to guarantee a Fascist majority in parliament
- Create his dictatorship, removing free elections, political opposition and the power of parliament

This chapter will examine the key issue of whether the dictatorship was created through the skill of Mussolini or was the result of the weakness and ineptitude of non-Fascist politicians. The issue is addressed through the following themes:

- Mussolini's increasing power 1922–4
- Electoral reform
- The creation of the Fascist dictatorship 1924–8

Key dates

1922	October	Mussolini appointed Prime Minister in a coalition government
	November	Parliament gave Mussolini the right to rule by decree for a 12-month period
	December	Creation of the Grand Council of Fascism strengthened Mussolini's control of Fascist movement
1923	January	Fascist squads converted into a national militia
	July	Parliament passed the Acerbo law, changing the electoral system to ensure that the most popular party was guaranteed a majority of MPs
1924	April	First general election under the Acerbo law gave Fascists a majority in parliament
	June	Murder of Matteotti, a leading Socialist, by Fascist thugs created a

		crisis for Mussolini and led to the emergence of a dictatorship
	July	Press censorship introduced
1925	January	Mussolini announced intention of creating a dictatorship
	December	Opposition political parties and free trade unions banned
1926	January	Mussolini gained the right to make laws without needing the approval of parliament

1 | Mussolini's Increasing Power 1922–4

Key question
What tactics did Mussolini use to increase his power?

Key date
Mussolini appointed Prime Minister in a coalition government: October 1922

On 30 October 1922 Mussolini arrived in Rome and was appointed Prime Minister of Italy. His Fascist blackshirts were now permitted to enter the city and they paraded in triumph before their leader.

Mussolini held the top political post in the land, but his dream of complete, unchallenged personal power was still a long way from realisation. Although many of his blackshirts believed that the Fascist revolution was about to begin, their leader showed caution. He had a more realistic appreciation of the limits of Fascist power. Mussolini was aware that a completely Fascist government was not yet possible – Fascism and its supporters did not have a majority of MPs in parliament and the King, no doubt supported by the army, would probably not allow him to do away with parliament. The new Prime Minister would have to construct a coalition government.

Mussolini's first government contained 14 senior ministers of whom only four were Fascists, the majority being Liberals and *Popolari*. This reassured those conservatives and Liberals who saw Fascism simply as a useful tool with which to crush the Left. They had supported the Fascist entry into government on these grounds and believed that once the Socialists had been destroyed they could either absorb Fascism into the regime or dispense with it altogether. Many thought that since Fascism lacked a coherent ideology and a clear set of policies it was unlikely to last for long.

Mussolini's strategy

Mussolini was determined to be no-one's pawn. Fascists might be a minority in the governing coalition but he held not only the post of Prime Minister but also the powerful positions of Minister of the Interior and Minister of Foreign Affairs. Above all, Mussolini was determined not to lose the momentum built up by the 'march on Rome' (see page 34). He was not yet able to secure supreme power, but he continued to use the threat of Fascist violence to intimidate parliament. At the same time he attempted to persuade MPs that, if they granted him near-dictatorial powers, they would be acting both in their own interests and in the interests of Italy itself.

Mussolini (at head of the table) at his first Cabinet meeting, 16 November 1922.

Mussolini tried to convince MPs that the breakdown of law and order was so serious and the threat of a Socialist revolution so great that extraordinary measures were needed to deal with the situation. He argued that, once the condition of the country had been stabilised, he would give up his special powers and revert to normal parliamentary rule. Of course, the Socialist threat was nearly non-existent and the collapse of law and order was largely the result of Fascist violence, but conservatives and Liberals remained mesmerised by the supposed danger from the left. They also genuinely believed Mussolini's assurances that any new powers they granted him would only be temporary.

Most MPs would remain convinced, until at least late 1924, that Mussolini could be 'transformed' into a respectable, even traditional, Prime Minister and that his movement could be found a place within the regime. This was to prove a fatal miscalculation. By the time these politicians realised their error it was already too late – the dictatorship was largely in place, parliament was increasingly an irrelevance, and open opposition was extremely hazardous.

Rule by decree

The new Prime Minister took immediate action to increase his power, demanding that parliament grant him the right to rule by decree for 12 months. This would mean that he could effectively create new laws without consulting parliament. Mussolini justified this demand by stating that only a strong government could take the stern measures that were necessary to restore law and order and to put the country back on its feet. To convince parliament to give him these extraordinary powers, he delivered a speech that was carefully designed to stress the military strength of Fascism, but at the same time to reassure the MPs that he was not about to overthrow the state or to introduce a set of radical policies:

> I am here to defend ... the revolution of the 'blackshirts' ... With 300,000 young men, fully armed, ... and prepared to obey any command of mine, I could have punished all those who have slandered the *Fascisti* ... I could have shut up parliament and formed a government of *Fascisti* exclusively; I could have done so, but I did not wish to do so, at any rate at the moment.
>
> I have formed a coalition government in order to gather in support of the suffering nation all those who, over and above questions of party, wish to save her.
>
> I thank all those who have worked with me ... [and] ... I pay a warm tribute to our King, who, by refusing ... to proclaim martial law, has avoided civil war and allowed the fresh and ardent *Fascisti* to pour itself into the sluggish mainstream of the State.
>
> Before arriving here we were asked on all sides for a programme. It is not, alas, programmes that are wanting in Italy, but men to carry them out. All the problems of Italian life have long since been solved on paper; but the will to put these solutions into practice has been lacking. The government today represents that firm and decisive will.

The MPs gave him a massive vote of confidence and granted him emergency powers for the 12-month period. Only the Socialists and Communists opposed the motion – prominent Liberals including Giolitti, Salandra and Facta proclaimed their support for this decisive new Prime Minister.

Grand Council of Fascism

Mussolini now moved to consolidate his position. In December he tried to increase his authority over his own party by establishing the **Grand Council of Fascism**.

Mussolini gave himself the right to make all appointments to the Grand Council to ensure that he alone controlled Fascist policy. In the following month he reduced the influence of provincial Fascist leaders still further by converting the Fascist squads into a **national militia** paid for by the state. He now possessed a private army of over 30,000 men, which he continued to use to intimidate potential opponents.

Support from powerful groups

Mussolini encouraged Fascist violence to deter potential opponents, but he also actively courted influential groups. By early 1923 he had persuaded the employers' organisation, *Confindustria*, to support his premiership.

Mussolini's government's decision not to attack widespread tax evasion had helped to convince industrialists that the new Prime Minister was no dangerous radical.

Mussolini even managed to gain some support from the Church by confirming that he intended to ban contraception and to make religious education compulsory in state schools. In response, the Pope began to withdraw support from the *Popolari*, to the point of instructing its leader, the priest Don Sturzo, to leave Italy. By mid-1923 the *Popolari* had been dropped from the governing coalition and had lost the backing of conservative Catholics. Its political significance was now effectively at an end.

Key dates

Creation of the Grand Council of Fascism strengthened Mussolini's control of Fascist movement: December 1922

Fascist squads converted into a national militia: January 1923

2 | Electoral Reform

Now that he was confident of the solid support of conservatives, many Catholics and the majority of Liberals, Mussolini moved to change the electoral system. He intended that this change would make his Fascists the biggest party in parliament.

Key question
How did electoral reform work to Mussolini's advantage?

Acerbo law

Mussolini proposed that the political party winning the most votes in a general election (provided it polled at least a quarter of the votes cast) should get two-thirds of the seats in the chamber of deputies. This was a revolutionary idea. Mussolini defended it by stating that the reform would produce a government which could count on the support of a large majority of MPs and which could then deal decisively with Italy's problems. There would be no more weak coalition governments where the different parties in the government could not agree what to do. It was these coalitions, so Mussolini claimed, that had plagued Liberal Italy and helped to bring the country to its knees. Of course, the Prime Minister neglected to point out that if his proposal became law the Fascists and their supporters would be the ones with the large majority of MPs and it would become virtually impossible to vote them out of power. Given the command, the Fascist squads would smash up the offices of hostile newspapers and would physically prevent opposition voters from reaching the polling booths. As Mussolini was Minister of the Interior, he could instruct the police to stand aside as Fascists caused havoc. The potential to fix elections was increased by the fact that he had promoted Fascist sympathisers to important positions in local government.

When this '**Acerbo law**' was debated in parliament in July 1923 it secured an overwhelming majority. The fact that armed blackshirts had roamed the chamber during the debate undoubtedly intimidated MPs, but the support for Mussolini's proposal was not simply the result of fear. Many MPs genuinely approved of the repressive actions taken by the government against what they still viewed as the dangerous, revolutionary left. They were prepared to turn a blind eye towards arrests and beatings of Socialists. Other MPs welcomed the end of those seemingly impotent coalition governments that Italy had experienced since the end of the war. However, the most

Acerbo law
Mussolini's reform of elections to guarantee a Fascist victory.

Key term

important factor was the continuing belief that Mussolini and his Fascists were not enemies of parliamentary government and that 'normality' would be restored as soon as circumstances permitted. Mussolini had assured the chamber on more than one occasion that he had no desire to dispense with parliament. The fact that he was the head of a coalition government and was prepared to discuss an electoral alliance with conservative groups seemed proof of his good faith. Giolitti and Salandra pledged their support for the reform, and were joined by the great majority of Liberals.

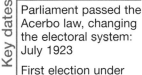

Key dates

Parliament passed the Acerbo law, changing the electoral system: July 1923

First election under the Acerbo law gave Fascists a majority in parliament: April 1924

Key term

Ballot-rigging
Fixing the result of an election by such illegal measures as destroying votes cast for opposition parties or adding fraudulent voting papers.

1924 Election

The new Acerbo law was put into practice in April 1924. In the general election of that month the Fascists campaigned with right-wing Liberals including Salandra. The Fascists and their allies secured 66 per cent of the vote. Fascist MPs increased from 35 to 374, giving the party a clear majority in the 535-seat chamber. Mussolini had certainly grown in public popularity, but widespread blackshirt violence and Fascist **ballot-rigging** had contributed significantly to the party's vote. Yet, despite the intimidation, the opposition parties – principally the Socialists and Communists – had still managed to attract 2.5 million votes. The resilience of support for opposition parties was illustrated by the fact that the two major cities in the north – Milan and Turin – both failed to produce Fascist majorities.

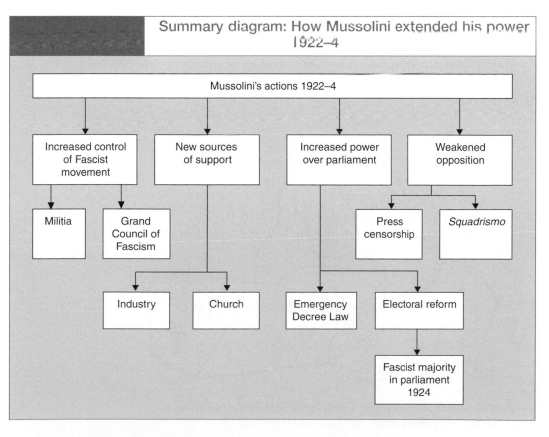

Summary diagram: How Mussolini extended his power 1922–4

3 | The Creation of the Fascist Dictatorship 1924–8

Key question
How was Mussolini able to make himself dictator?

It now seemed that Mussolini had control of parliament, but he still did not possess the powers of a dictator. Parliament was still needed to approve laws, opposition parties still existed, and the King could still sack his Prime Minister. It was unclear whether Mussolini would try to establish a dictatorship or how he would do it. In the event, the murder of a prominent opponent would threaten Mussolini's very survival but also pave the way to a Fascist dictatorship.

Murder of Matteotti

When parliament reopened, opposition MPs tried to publicise illegal Fascist actions at the polls. Their most prominent spokesman, the Socialist Giacomo Matteotti, produced evidence detailing Fascist violence and terror during the election campaign. On 10 June 1924, within days of these allegations being made, Fascist thugs abducted Matteotti in broad daylight and stabbed him to death. This brutal murder shocked not only Mussolini's political enemies but also many pro-Mussolini Liberals who thought that the Fascists had finally gone too far. Mussolini denied all knowledge of the crime but, as evidence linking the Prime Minister to the murder began to appear in the press, public opinion began to turn against him. At this point, opposition MPs walked out of parliament and set up their own breakaway parliament. These MPs, mainly Socialist, Communist and dissident *Popolari*, hoped that their '**Aventine secession**' (named after a similar event in ancient Rome) might encourage the King to dismiss Mussolini. The Fascist leader's position appeared vulnerable.

Key date
Murder of Matteotti, a leading Socialist, by Fascist thugs created a crisis for Mussolini: June 1924

Key term
Aventine secession
Anti-Fascist MPs walked out of parliament in protest against Fascist violence, hoping that this would encourage the King to sack Mussolini.

An anti-Fascist Italian newspaper's view of Mussolini trying to 'keep the lid on' the Matteotti affair, 1924.

Key terms

Press censorship
Newspapers were
no longer
permitted to
criticise the Fascist
government.

Leggi Fascistissime
All opposition
parties and
organisations
banned.

Free trade unions
Trade unions which
represented the
interests of workers,
and which were
independent of
government or
Fascist control.

Key dates

Press censorship
introduced: July 1924

Mussolini announced
intention of creating a
dictatorship: January
1925

Opposition parties
and free trade unions
banned: December
1925

The King refused to contemplate the dismissal of Mussolini,
fearing that such a decision would only strengthen the
revolutionary left and might lead to civil war. He was encouraged
in this belief by leading Liberals and conservatives who saw the
affair not as an opportunity to dispose of the Fascist leader, but
rather as a chance to increase their influence over the weakened
Prime Minister. Giolitti and Salandra, for example, still supported
Mussolini's premiership. For such men there appeared at that
moment to be no viable acceptable alternative to the Fascist
leader.

Destruction of democracy

While his position was being supported by these conservative
groups, Mussolini moved to prevent any further opposition.

In July 1924 he introduced **press censorship** and in the
following month banned meetings by opposition political parties.
But, despite the government's efforts, the controversy raised by
the Matteotti affair did not disappear. Those Liberal leaders who
had previously supported the government joined the opposition
in November in protest against press censorship. Eventually, in
December 1924, leading Fascists, exasperated by the uncertainty
created by the affair and frustrated by the government's lack of
radicalism, presented Mussolini with an ultimatum. If he did not
end the Matteotti affair immediately and move decisively towards
the establishment of a dictatorship, they would withdraw their
support.

The Prime Minister bowed to their demands and, in a speech
on 3 January 1925, told parliament that he accepted
responsibility for all Fascist actions up to that date:

> I declare before all Italy that I assume full responsibility for what
> has happened ... If Fascism has turned out to be only castor oil
> and rubber truncheons instead of being a superb passion inspiring
> the best youth of Italy, I am responsible ... Italians want peace and
> quiet, and to get on with its [*sic*.] work. I shall give it all these, if
> possible in love, but if necessary by force.

He was signalling that he would now take the measures necessary
to give himself much greater personal power. His speech was
cheered in the chamber. With a clear majority in parliament and
confident that the King would not move against him, Mussolini
created his dictatorship. What opposition there was in the
chamber proved no threat – it was divided, lacking in leadership
and compromised by its earlier support for Fascism.

In January 1925 the Prime Minister established a committee to
reform the constitution. In December the *Leggi Fascistissime* were
passed, banning opposition political parties and **free trade
unions**.

Press censorship was tightened, a new secret police was set up,
and a special court was established to try political crimes. Fascist
control of local government was increased by replacing elected
mayors with nominated officials, known as *podestas*.

In January 1926 Mussolini was granted the right to issue decrees carrying the full force of law. He could now make laws without consulting parliament, which meant his personal rule was enshrined in law. By the end of the year parliament had even lost the right to debate proposed laws or criticise the government.

Final touches to the dictatorship were added in 1928 when the King lost the right to select the Prime Minister. In future, a list of possible candidates would be drawn up by the Grand Council of Fascism, a body appointed and controlled by Mussolini, and the King would have to make his selection from this list.

> **Key date**
>
> Mussolini gained the right to make laws without needing the approval of parliament: January 1926

Summary diagram: The creation of the Fascist dictatorship 1924–8

```
                          Mussolini's actions
                                 │
            ┌────────────────────┴────────────────────┐
            ▼                                          ▼
  Control of government and parliament        Destruction of opposition
            │                                          │
     ┌──────┴──────┐                    ┌──────────────┼──────────────┐
     ▼             ▼                    ▼              ▼              ▼
 King lost      Rule by             Trade        Opposition      Stronger
 right to       decree              unions        parties         press
 select                             banned        banned        censorship
 Prime Minister
```

Study Guide: AS Questions

In the style of AQA

Read the following source and then answer the questions that follow.

Adapted from: R. Thurlow, Fascism, *1999.*

Fascism began with leader worship and political thuggery directed at the supposed Communist threat. It then developed an extreme nationalist ideology.

(a) What is meant by 'political thuggery' in relation to the coming to power of the Fascists in Italy?   (3 marks)

(b) Explain why the blackshirts became an important force in Italy in the years 1918–29.   (7 marks)

(c) 'A dictatorship was quickly and fully consolidated.' With reference to Fascist Italy by 1929, explain why you agree or disagree with this statement.   (15 marks)

Source: AQA, June 2003

Exam tips
The cross-references are intended to take you straight to the material that will help you to answer the questions.

(a) It is important that you get your timing right in these multi-part questions. You will have 45 minutes to answer all three parts, so try not to spend more than five minutes on (a) and 12–13 minutes on (b). In question (a) you must give examples of Fascist 'political thuggery' in the years 1919–22, when the violence of Fascist squads in the countryside and towns of central-northern Italy made Fascism a political force (pages 27–31). You should also give examples of 'thuggery' after Mussolini had come to power in 1922, such as the murder of Matteotti (pages 50–1).

(b) Your answer should not just include examples of blackshirt violence, it must also explain why this violence helped Mussolini to come to power in 1922. For example, squad violence in the countryside attracted new recruits to Fascism (pages 26–8) and blackshirt pressure for a march on Rome created the political crisis of October 1922 (pages 34–6). You must also examine the role of the blackshirts in the emergence of the dictatorship, and for this you will need to read not just Chapter 4 but also Chapter 5 (pages 67–8).

(c) A plan is vital for this question. You should first define what is meant by the dictatorship (pages 50–2). You must then plan your answers to both elements of the question – was the dictatorship established 'quickly'? and was the dictatorship 'fully consolidated' by 1929? It is the second question that will form the major part of your essay and you will have to refer not only to this chapter (pages 50–2) but also to Chapter 5 (pages 57–65). It is essential that you make a judgement on this question and justify it:
- By 1929 did Mussolini have the ability to make his own laws without needing parliament?
- Was his position entirely secure within the state and the Fascist party, with no threat of dismissal and no meaningful opposition?

In the style of Edexcel

1. Why did Mussolini's power survive the Matteotti crisis?
(20 marks)

Source: Edexcel, May 2002

2. Why were the democratic parties unable to prevent the establishment of a Fascist dictatorship in the years 1924–5? (40 marks)

Source: Edexcel, May 2002
Edexcel Ltd, accepts no responsibility whatsoever for the accuracy or method of working in the answers given.

Exam tips

The cross-references are intended to take you straight to the material that will help you to answer the questions.

1. In question **1** it is important that you do not simply outline the events from the death of Matteotti to the establishment of the dictatorship. Instead, you should identify and explain those factors that helped Mussolini to keep his majority in parliament and avoid dismissal by the King. Your plan should include the following headings, each of which deserves at least one paragraph:

    *   Why the murder of Matteotti was a potential threat to Mussolini (pages 50–1).
    *   The reasons why key Liberals did not try to persuade the King to dismiss Mussolini (pages 51–2).
    *   The reasons why the King was reluctant to dismiss Mussolini (pages 51–2).
    *   The actions Mussolini took against opponents and to increase his own power (pages 50–2).

    In your conclusion you should try to identify the most important one or two reasons why Mussolini survived the Matteotti crisis. You should also point out how the factors linked together: Mussolini's own actions together with the indecisiveness of the opposition helped to ensure his survival.

2. In question **2** you should identify what is meant by the 'democratic parties', and here you will need to look at your notes from both this and the preceding chapter. To help to assess the reasons why these parties were unable to prevent a Fascist dictatorship you could draw up the following table:

Democratic party	Size in parliament and country	Party weaknesses	Action or inaction of party 1924–5	Mussolini's actions 1924–5
Liberals	Page 29	Pages 23, 31, 39	Pages 49–52	Pages 49–52
Socialists	Page 29	Page 18	Pages 49–52	Pages 49–52
Catholic *Popolari*	Page 29	Page 48	Pages 49–52	Pages 49–52

Before writing your answer you will need to decide which of these parties had the greatest capacity to prevent a Fascist dictatorship. If you decide that it was the Liberals then you should begin your answer with your analysis of why the Liberals were unable to prevent the dictatorship. Was it the result of their own weaknesses and mistakes or was it more to do with the actions of Mussolini? You can then move on to a discussion of the failure of the other parties.

In the style of OCR

Assess the reasons why there was little effective opposition to Mussolini's consolidation of power between 1922 and 1928.

(45 marks)

Exam tips

The cross-references are intended to take you straight to the material that will help you to answer the question.

One way of approaching this question is to consider potential sources of opposition to Mussolini and to analyse why these groups did not resist the consolidation of power more effectively. The following table will help you.

Potential sources of opposition	Actions taken by Mussolini to reassure or gain support from this group	Actions taken by Mussolini to remove or crush opposition	Other reasons for lack of effective opposition	Examples of opposition to Mussolini's consolidation of power
Liberals	Speeches (page 47). Rule by decree (pages 46–7)	Banning of opposition parties (page 51)	Acerbo law (page 48)	Aventine secession (page 50)
Socialists and trade unions	–	Murder of Matteotti (pages 50–1). Squad violence (pages 28–31). Free trade unions banned (page 51)	See Chapter 3 (page 18)	Matteotti's exposure of Fascist electoral fraud (pages 50–1). Votes in 1924 election (page 49)
Catholics	Education and contraception (page 48)	Pressure on Pope to remove support for *Popolari* (page 48)	See Chapter 3 (page 48)	Aventine secession (page 50)
King	See Chapter 5 (page 61)	See Chapter 5 (page 61)	–	–
Industrialists	Taxation (page 48) and see Chapter 6 (page 82)	–	–	–
Media	See Chapter 5 (page 58)	Press censorship (page 51)	–	See Chapter 5 (pages 67–8)
Fascist *Ras*	See Chapter 5 (pages 63–5)	Grand Council of Fascism (page 47)	–	–

The table will help you to plan your answer, but it is important that you point out the links between factors. For example, the Socialists were certainly opposed to Mussolini's actions but lack of unity within Socialism made it easier for Mussolini to use repression against them. It is also vital that you explain what you consider to be the main reasons for the lack of effective opposition – was it simply the use of violence and repression, or was it Mussolini's tactics and reassuring claims, or was it the naivety of the opposition?

5

Mussolini and the Fascist Political System

POINTS TO CONSIDER

There are three distinct parts to this chapter. The first part examines the nature and extent of Mussolini's dictatorship, while the second addresses the question of why there was not more opposition to Fascist rule. The final section considers both the similarities between Fascist Italy and Nazi Germany and the key differences. These themes are examined under the following headings:

- Mussolini's aim: personal dictatorship
- Propaganda and the cult of personality
- Mussolini and government
- Mussolini and powerful groups in Italian society
- Mussolini and the Fascist Party
- Relations between Party and State
- Popular support and opposition
- Comparison of Fascism and Nazism

Key dates

1925	Last congress of Fascist Party: Mussolini banned internal arguments
	Vidoni Palace Pact outlawed independent trade unions
1926	Mussolini able to make laws without the consent of parliament
	Parliament lost right to debate proposed laws or to criticise the government
	Opposition newspapers suppressed
	Cult of personality underway
1928	All appointments in Fascist Party made by Party headquarters in Rome, controlled by Mussolini
1929	Lateran Agreements improved relations between Fascism and Catholic Church
1933	Hitler became Chancellor of Germany
1939	Parliament replaced by the Chamber of Fasces and Corporations

Key question
What was meant by 'personal dictatorship'?

Key date

Mussolini able to make laws without the consent of parliament: 1926

1 | Mussolini's Aim: Personal Dictatorship

By 1926 Mussolini had achieved his ambition of becoming dictator of Italy. He could make laws simply by issuing decrees. Parliament was under his full control – no longer a forum for debate, but simply a theatre in which his decisions could be applauded by Fascist supporters and sympathisers. With Liberals and *Popolari* divided and leaderless and the Socialists under constant physical attack, organised political opposition did not exist. Of course, technically, Mussolini could still be dismissed by the King, but the 'march on Rome' and the 'Matteotti affair' (pages 34 and 50–1) had proved that Victor Emmanuel was not prepared to stand up to his Prime Minister. Furthermore, providing the King remained in fear and awe of the Fascist leader, Mussolini need not worry about the armed forces, as they were very unlikely to break their pledge of loyalty to the monarch.

With his position secure, Mussolini now set out to create his Fascist state. This state was to be a personal dictatorship, for the Prime Minister's central goal was to maintain and increase his own personal power. In pursuit of this aim he encouraged a cult of personality that stressed his genius, his power and his indispensability as leader of the nation. He attempted to consolidate his position by seeking a constructive working relationship with powerful interest groups, notably the Church, industrialists and the armed forces.

Mussolini's pursuit of personal power took priority over the desire to impose Fascist ideas on all aspects of Italian life. This policy disappointed many in the Fascist Party who hoped that the Fascist revolution would sweep away interest groups and create a state in which the Party controlled all areas of government. Their leader still talked of revolution, but he was determined that the Party should be his servant and not his master. Mussolini would decide what powers the Party should possess, what Fascist policy should be, and how and when it should be implemented.

The Italy that Mussolini created was one in which he alone possessed ultimate power. Interest groups, the old institutions of government and the Fascist Party all competed against each other for authority, but they looked to Mussolini to adjudicate their disputes and to make the final decisions. Without him government could not function and the regime would collapse.

Key question
What was the purpose of Fascist propaganda?

Key date

Opposition newspapers suppressed: 1926

2 | Propaganda and the Cult of Personality

Mussolini had first come to national attention as the editor of a propagandist newspaper, *Il Popolo d'Italia*, and was determined to use propaganda to build up support for his regime and to deter opposition. Not surprisingly he was anxious to control the news. In 1926 opposition newspapers were suppressed, and journalists and their editors made aware that they could be arrested if they published anything derogatory towards the regime. Mussolini's own press office issued 'official' versions of events which newspapers were expected to publish without question.

Radio and cinema were also to be tools for Fascist propaganda. There were perhaps only 40,000 radios in the whole of Italy in the mid-1920s, but from 1924 the radio network was run by the state. News bulletins continually praised Mussolini and broadcast his speeches in full. Radios were given to schools and by the 1930s the Party was trying to ensure that even those living in rural areas could at least listen to communal radios in their villages. The regime was slow to make propagandist feature films, and American 'Hollywood' films always dominated Italian cinema screens, but each of these films would be preceded by a short newsreel which gave a Fascist version of current events.

Cult of personality

The media were to play a crucial role in creating the cult of '*il Duce*', as Mussolini was increasingly known. The cult was intended to build popular support for the dictator and to overawe potential opponents by stressing his supposed superhuman talents. He was to be portrayed not as just another politician but as Italy's saviour, a man chosen by destiny to save the country from the Socialist menace and corrupt democratic politicians and to restore Italian greatness. He was the new Caesar – a man of genius, a man of action, a man of culture, a statesman of world renown dedicated only to the revival of Italy.

> **Key question**
> What was the cult of personality? How successful was it?

Mussolini viewing a statue of Julius Caesar that had been installed in the recently excavated Roman Forum. Why would Mussolini want to associate himself with memories of Ancient Rome?

Key date

Cult of personality
underway: 1926

By 1926 the regime was using all the methods of propaganda at its disposal to convey its message. Government-controlled newspapers stressed Mussolini's benevolence and took particular pride in quoting the opinions of foreign admirers, particularly if they were leading statesmen. The British Foreign Secretary, Austen Chamberlain, was thus widely reported as saying that Mussolini was 'a wonderful man working for the greatness of his country', while Winston Churchill's opinion in 1927 that the *Duce*'s 'sole thought was the lasting well-being of the Italian people as he sees it' received similar publicity. Mussolini's supposed dedication to duty led to stories that he toiled for up to 20 hours per day on government business. In fact, the light was left on in his study for most of the night to back up this claim and to disguise the fact that the dictator usually retired to bed rather early.

The newspapers also suggested that the *Duce* was infallible. 'Mussolini is always right' became a popular phrase, an idea the dictator encouraged with such utterances as 'often I would like to be wrong, but so far it has never happened and events have always turned out just as I foresaw'. To maintain this impression, Mussolini was quick to claim the credit for any successes and still quicker to blame others for any mistakes.

The *Duce* was keen to be portrayed as a vigorous, athletic and courageous man – a model for all Italian males. Magazines and newspapers printed pictures of his horse-riding, enjoying winter sports, driving cars at high speed and flying airplanes. An image

A 1927 photograph of Mussolini playing the violin. Propaganda photographs of the supposed myriad talents of the *Duce* were distributed to newspapers and magazines both in Italy and abroad.

of youthfulness was maintained by the suppression of any references to his age or to the fact that he needed to wear glasses.

Not content with this, the dictator insisted that he must also be seen as a man of culture. Consequently it was made known that he had read and digested all 35 volumes of the Italian Encyclopaedia and had read nearly all the classics of European literature, including the complete works of William Shakespeare. Fascist propagandists also claimed that Mussolini was an accomplished musician.

Mussolini's expectation that everyone would be taken in by this image and these exaggerated claims revealed his own vanity and also his low opinion of the public. Indeed, he declared that the public 'are stupid, dirty, do not work hard enough and are content with their little cinema shows'. Mussolini believed that the masses were not really interested in debate or discussion but preferred to be told what to do. They would enjoy the belief that they were ruled by a near superman and would feel proud that Italy was apparently so admired by the rest of the world. Spectacles, parades and constant propaganda would keep their interest and secure their allegiance. As Mussolini put it, 'one must always know how to strike the imagination of the public: that is the real secret of how to govern'.

S. E. BENITO MUSSOLINI

What impression of Mussolini is this poster trying to convey? Note the symbols of Ancient Rome.

It is uncertain how many people were impressed by the 'Cult of *Ducismo*'. Many, perhaps most, must have been extremely sceptical, but the cult did help to convince large numbers of Italians that there was no conceivable alternative to the Fascist regime. The sheer volume of propaganda stressing Mussolini's power and genius deterred potential opposition. To this extent the cult of personality certainly achieved its aim.

3 | Mussolini and Government

Key question
What were the roles of the King, ministers, and parliament?

Mussolini was determined to ensure that all real power rested in his hands – he alone would devise policy and he alone would make all major decisions. The King would be an irrelevance and cabinet, parliament and the institutions of state would be his loyal servants.

Role of the King
King Victor Emmanuel was easily dealt with. The monarchy had traditionally distanced itself from domestic policy and concerned itself principally with foreign affairs. Mussolini realised that he completely overawed Victor Emmanuel, and took advantage of this to deter the monarchy from any political involvement. The dictator still followed protocol by visiting the King twice a week, but Victor Emmanuel was never asked for his advice and was only told what Mussolini wanted him to hear.

Role of government ministers
Mussolini was not prepared to share power with his ministers. There would be no Cabinet-style government with ministers jointly discussing and deciding government policy. There was to be no government 'team'. Instead, the role of ministers was simply to follow the *Duce*'s instructions unquestioningly. In fact, Mussolini himself held the most important ministries – foreign affairs, interior and the three armed services – for the greater part of his time as dictator.

Key dates

Parliament lost the right to debate proposed laws or criticise the government: 1926

Parliament abolished and replaced by equally powerless Chamber of Fasces and Corporations: 1939

Role of parliament
The *Duce* had even less regard for parliament. By 1926 it had lost its ability to discuss policy, to debate and amend proposed legislation, and to criticise the government. Its reputation and political significance was to sink still further in subsequent years. With opposition parties banned, the chamber was dominated by sycophantic Fascist deputies who did not even bother to vote formally on Mussolini's legislation: they simply shouted their assent. Free elections ceased to exist. The electorate was reduced to exclude most of the working classes, who had previously supported the Socialists. In addition, all candidates had to be approved by the Fascists, and the results were shamelessly rigged to show over 98 per cent approval for the regime. Eventually, in January 1939, parliament abolished itself altogether, to be replaced by the equally meaningless Chamber of Fasces and Corporations.

Gaining the support of the civil service

If the Cabinet and parliament were to be Mussolini's servants then so, too, were the other institutions of the Italian state – the **civil service**, local government, the judiciary and the armed services. However, he was keen to achieve his goals without provoking the head-on clash with these institutions that the radicals in the Fascist Party desired. A wholesale sacking of personnel in the civil service, judiciary and army officer corps and their replacement by Fascist Party appointees would almost certainly have caused a crisis. Mussolini wanted to avoid any such crisis and was anxious to restrict the power of the Party and to keep it under his complete command. The dictator recognised that the conservatives, who were prominent in state institutions, were largely sympathetic towards him, if distrustful of the Party radicals. He set out to capitalise on this sympathy by using his powers of **patronage** to reward loyalty and by introducing policies that conservatives could support. However, at the same time, he made it clear that if his wishes were not supported and obeyed, he would be ruthless in seeking out and destroying opposition.

Mussolini's approach meant that there was no Fascist revolution in government. Indeed, the Fascist Party complained that Party membership was dangerously low in the institutions of state. In 1927, for instance, it was estimated that only about 15 per cent of the civil service was Fascist. Nevertheless, the civil service loyally carried out the instructions of its political master, the *Duce*. During the 1930s, Fascist Party membership did increase among civil servants, but this seems to have been largely the result of a recognition that promotion depended on being a card-carrying supporter of the regime.

Gaining support in the armed forces

The dictator adopted a similar policy in his dealings with the armed services. Mussolini emphasised that he and the military shared a common interest in expanding the armed forces and in pursuing an aggressive foreign policy. Further support was gained by promoting senior generals to the prestigious post of Field Marshal. Ambitious officers soon came to realise that a pro-Fascist attitude, and preferably Party membership, would enormously enhance their prospects of promotion. The army did, admittedly, resent the pretensions of the Fascist militia to be a significant military force, but it was still willing to give its loyalty to the *Duce*.

Controlling the judges

Only with the judiciary did Mussolini conduct a purge of what he considered to be undesirable elements. Dozens of judges were sacked for being insufficiently sympathetic towards Fascism or for being too independent of the government. The dictator wanted to ensure that the judiciary could be relied on to follow his government's instructions. The Italian legal system consequently lost all claim to impartiality. Imprisonment without trial became commonplace and, where cases did come to court, Mussolini occasionally intervened to dictate verdicts and sentences.

Key question
How did Mussolini attempt to win the support of key groups in the Italian state: civil service, armed forces, judges, local government?

Key terms

Civil service
Civil servants advise government ministers on policy and ensure that government policies are carried out.

Patronage
The use of appointments and promotions to reward support.

Controlling local government

This determination to control all the institutions of state also extended to local government. Local self-government was abolished and elected mayors and town councils were replaced by officials appointed from Rome.

Mussolini's methods ensured that he extended his power throughout the Italian state, building up support based on self-interest and avoiding unnecessary conflict. His tactics in pursuit of his goal of complete personal power varied between aggression and conciliation, according to the nature of the institution in question.

Key question
How did Mussolini seek to gain the support of key groups in Italian society: the Church and industrialists?

4| Mussolini and Powerful Groups in Italian Society

Mussolini adopted a broadly conciliatory approach when dealing with those interest groups whose support he needed to consolidate his regime: the Church and industry.

The *Duce* had wooed the Vatican even before he became Prime Minister, disavowing his earlier anti-clericalism (see page 22) and emphasising that the Church had nothing to fear from Fascism. Mussolini also pointed out that Fascism and Catholicism faced common enemies in Socialism and Liberalism. Relations steadily warmed and in 1929 the Lateran Agreements were signed (see pages 97–8), finally healing the breach between the Catholic Church and the Italian state. Mussolini could now rely on official Catholic support for his regime.

Key dates
Lateran Agreements improved relations between Catholic Church and Fascism: 1929

Vidoni Palace Pact outlawed independent trade unions: 1925

Mussolini also adopted conciliatory tactics, at least to begin with, when dealing with Italian industrialists. In the Vidoni Palace Pact of 1925 all Socialist and Catholic trade unions were banned and, in the following year, strikes were outlawed. A fuller discussion of Fascism's policy towards industry is to be found on pages 82–7, but these early concessions were instrumental in securing industrialists' loyalty to the regime.

Key question
How did Mussolini cement his control over the Fascist Party?

5 | Mussolini and the Fascist Party

Once he was in power, Mussolini had to decide what should be the role of his National Fascist Party (PNF). Should the PNF play a key role in the Fascist state or should Mussolini simply use government departments to bring about change? Should the PNF be a mass party or a disciplined élite? The *Duce* seems to have found it difficult to decide on these questions and his opinion varied over the years. However, his mind was clear and his policy unchanging on the question of the relationship between the leader and the Party – the PNF would serve the *Duce* and not vice versa.

From the time of the Fascist breakthrough into Italian politics in 1920–1, Mussolini had stressed the need for discipline and central control. However, his struggle to assert his leadership had not been easy. Local Fascist leaders (*Ras*) acknowledged Mussolini as the *Duce* of Fascism, but they were reluctant to accept central direction. In fact, their violent actions during 1921 and 1922 at times embarrassed a leader who was trying to reassure conservatives that his movement was a dynamic yet responsible political force. The 'march on Rome' (page 34) was at least in part a concession to pressure from the radical *squadristi*.

Once he had been appointed Prime Minister, Mussolini moved to extend his control over his Party. The creation of the militia provided paid employment for Fascist *squadristi* and helped to ensure their continued loyalty. The establishment of the Grand Council of Fascism (page 47) as the supreme policy-making body for the movement strengthened the leader's position still further since he appointed all of its members. As he rewarded loyalty, so he punished opposition – during 1923 local parties were purged of active or potential dissidents. Despite these efforts, Mussolini's control over the Party was still not absolute, as the *Ras* (page 51) demonstrated when, during the Matteotti crisis of 1924, they demanded that he establish a dictatorship.

If the *Ras* and their *squadristi* hoped that the creation of a dictatorship would enhance Party power, they were to be disappointed. Mussolini set up a personal dictatorship. With control over the institutions of state, his power was secure and he was no longer vulnerable to pressure from within the PNF. The *Duce* illustrated his mastery of the Party at the last Party congress, held in June 1925. Mussolini demanded that the Party should end internal arguments and obey the orders of its leader. Dissenting voices were shouted down. Although it was scheduled to last three days, the convention lasted only a few hours.

Key dates

Final Fascist Party congress banned criticism of Mussolini from within the Party: 1925

All appointments in Fascist Party made by Party headquarters in Rome, controlled by Mussolini: 1928

By the end of 1928 the *Duce* had organised a further purge of Fascists suspected of disloyalty and had established the principle that all Party posts should be appointments made from Party headquarters in Rome, a headquarters that he controlled. The PNF had become totally subservient to its leader. The Grand Council of Fascism was under the complete control of the *Duce* and, as the years went by, he called it less and less frequently.

Divisions within the Fascist Party

That Mussolini had managed to achieve absolute dominance over Fascism was testament to his political skills, but it also showed that without Mussolini there was nothing to hold the Party together. The PNF was not a united, coherent movement but rather a broad, uneasy coalition of groups with differing views and priorities. *Squadristi* demanded the continuance of violent raids, ex-Socialists wanted the reorganisation of industry, nationalists desired the revision of the First World War peace settlement, and conservatives hoped for the restoration of law and order and normality. Only Mussolini could provide unity. The disparate, disorganised factions came to recognise this and looked to win his interest and support. The dictator's concerns and enthusiasms would change over the years, and he was sympathetic first to one faction then to another – initially conciliatory to the conservatives to secure the support of interest groups such as industry, then enthusiastic for a reorganisation of industry into a corporate state (pages 83–5), and in the late 1930s reverting to radical ideas of revolutionising Italian social habits. Of course, the

Key question
How did divisions within the party increase Mussolini's power?

real significance of this was that the *Duce* and not the Party would be responsible for determining the course of Fascist policy.

Preventing the emergence of rivals

Key question
How did Mussolini ensure that there were no credible rivals to his leadership?

Given the Party's subservience to its *Duce*, it was not surprising that the men who occupied senior posts within the Party were notable less for their ability than for their obedience and powers of flattery. The most senior post, that of Party Secretary, was held by a succession of utterly loyal Fascists of very modest ability. Under such men as Achille Starace, Party Secretary from 1931 to 1939, the PNF opened its doors to all those who saw Party membership simply as a way to secure a safe job in the Fascist administration. By the mid-1930s workers and peasants, who had once made up almost 30 per cent of Party membership, had become a tiny minority. The PNF now consisted overwhelmingly of white-collar state employees.

Mussolini's promotion of second-rate officials showed his susceptibility to flattery, but it also revealed his continuing concern to prevent the emergence of potential rivals. Men of drive and apparent ability found themselves moved far from the centre of power. For example, the young squad leader, Italo Balbo (see page 27) who achieved fame in 1931 when he completed a trans-Atlantic flight, was soon sent to occupy a post of luxurious idleness in Libya. Another young *squadrista*, Dino Grandi, apparently had some ambition to succeed the *Duce* but found himself despatched to London as Italian ambassador, a post of honour but of little power. No serious rival to the *Duce* ever emerged. Indeed, even men who had made their name as radical *squadristi*, such as Roberto Farinacci (page 28), enthusiastically joined in the cult of the *Duce*. They realised that Mussolini was prepared to allow them to keep much of their power in the provinces providing they remained utterly loyal and obedient to him. They were also well aware that without Mussolini as dictator their own power would collapse.

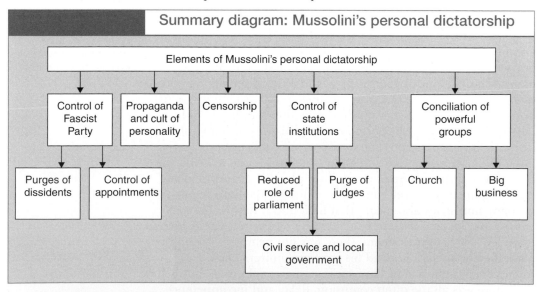

Summary diagram: Mussolini's personal dictatorship

6 | Relations between Party and State

Although the Party lost most of the dynamism it had once possessed and became a bloated bureaucracy offering secure, undemanding jobs to Fascist supporters, it still had a role in Mussolini's state. The *Duce* hoped that the Party would help to transform ordinary Italians into obedient, disciplined Fascists and, in pursuit of this, he gave it a significant role, particularly in the areas of education, leisure and propaganda.

The PNF therefore represented a rival authority to that of the institutions of the state, and there were tensions and arguments between Party organisations and government departments. For example, should the Fascist youth movement, the ONB, be controlled by the Party or by the government's Ministry of Education? A similar argument took place over the question of who should run the organisation for adult leisure activities, the *Dopolavoro* ('After work'). There was rivalry between the government economics ministry and the Fascist bureaucracy controlling the new Fascist corporations.

In the armed forces there was rivalry between the Fascist militia and the regular army, the latter resenting the claim that blackshirt officers were equal in status to army officers. The army and militia also argued over the distribution of weapons between them. Such rivalry was not confined to national politics – in fact it was particularly common in the provinces where local Party secretaries competed for power with provincial prefects who, according to the Ministry of the Interior in Rome, had responsibility for local government.

In these disputes over jurisdiction both sides looked to Mussolini to solve the disputes. This gave the *Duce* great power. For example, in 1927 he transferred control over the *Dopolavoro* organisation from the Ministry of National Economy to the Party. In contrast, in 1929, he took the youth organisation, the ONB, out of the hands of the Party organisation and handed control to the Ministry of National Education.

Key question
Why were there rivalries between the Party and government institutions and how did these rivalries increase Mussolini's power?

Effectiveness of Fascist government

Disputes between Party organisations and government departments made government slow and inefficient. With so many matters awaiting the *Duce*'s personal decision, delays were unavoidable, despite his spurious claims to be working up to 20 hours each day. The dictator's determination that he should personally occupy the most important ministries of state only worsened the situation. When decisions were taken they were often made without proper thought or consultation, as when the *Duce* selected the airforce's new fighter plane after only a most cursory glance at the relevant information. Mussolini's tenure of so many ministries also meant that he found it impossible to ensure that his decisions were actually being carried out as he had intended. Fascist government, then, was not nearly as streamlined and efficient as the *Duce* and his foreign admirers liked to suggest. Mussolini might have supreme personal power, but below him there was all too often confusion, delay and incompetence.

Key question
How efficient was Fascist government?

	Summary diagram: Tensions between the Fascist Party and government institutions

Causes of tension
- Role of Party not clearly defined by Mussolini
- Party responsibilities subject to change by Mussolini
- Ambitions of Fascist *Ras* to increase their power

Examples of tension
- Arguments between Party and Ministry of Education over control of Fascist youth movement, the ONB
- Arguments between Party and Ministry of National Economy over control of adult leisure organisation, *Dopolavoro*
- Arguments between Fascist militia and regular army over allocation of new weapons
- Arguments between local Party secretaries and prefects, appointed by Ministry of Interior, over control of local government

7 | Popular Support and Opposition

Key question
What problems did opponents of Fascism face?

Mussolini's control over the Fascist Party and the great institutions of state made open opposition both difficult and dangerous. As the death of Matteotti proved (page 50), the Duce had no compunction about using violence and even murder to silence his critics. By 1926 it is probable that Fascist squads had murdered around 2000 opponents. The ban on political activity outside the Fascist Party, together with the imposition of press censorship, denied opponents a platform for their views. Dissidents were spied upon by the dictator's secret police, the **OVRA**, severely beaten up, and often imprisoned without trial.

Key term

OVRA
Fascist secret police.

Anti-Fascist opposition

Key question
How much opposition was there to the Fascist regime?

Faced with such an array of repressive measures, it was not surprising that opposition within Italy was disorganised and ineffective. Only a small number of sizeable networks of anti-Fascists existed within the country. There were the Communists who tried to maintain an underground party organisation within Italy, published their own newspaper, *L'Unità*, and distributed anti-Fascist propaganda leaflets. It is estimated that they could count on no more than 7000 active supporters who were consistently harried by the regime. The prominent Marxist writer and founder of *L'Unità*, Antonio Gramsci, was sentenced to 20 years' imprisonment in 1927. His health destroyed, he died in 1937.

A second group was named Justice and Liberty. It was founded by Carlo Roselli, who had escaped from a Fascist prison in 1929 and settled in Paris. He hoped to create an alliance between

Socialists and Liberals opposed to the regime. From Paris, Justice and Liberty kept the international press informed about the repression and injustice within Italy, and smuggled leaflets to its supporters inside the country. In turn these supporters tried to spread anti-Fascist propaganda in Italian cities. Like the Communists, Justice and Liberty had only a few thousand supporters. Despite the movement's small scale it still attracted the full attention of the Fascist state: Roselli was murdered in 1937 by Fascists acting on instructions from the government in Rome.

A significant reason for the limited impact of opposition groups was that they squabbled among themselves and failed to form a common anti-Fascist front. For example, Italian exiles led by the Socialist Pietro Nenni formed the *Concentrazione Antifascista* in Paris in 1927. They produced a weekly newspaper called *La Libertá*. However, internal disputes and the refusal of Communist anti-Fascists to co-operate led to its dissolution in 1934.

Encouraging co-operation with Fascism

The lack of significant opposition within Italy was certainly a reflection of the strength of the regime's repressive machinery, but it was also proof that the dictator knew how to manipulate his subjects. Those Liberals and *Popolari* who had grown disillusioned with Fascism were usually left alone, providing they did not dare to criticise the regime openly. From time to time, a few individuals would be assaulted by the OVRA or the militia simply to remind others that conformity was the safest option.

Journalists and intellectuals who might have been expected vigorously to oppose a system that so enthusiastically suppressed individual freedoms were encouraged to join that system. Loyal journalists received extra pay in the form of government grants. Given the easy rewards and the apparent impossibility of publishing critical material, most writers settled for the role of Party hack or else avoided political journalism altogether. Mussolini offered similar inducements to academics and intellectuals. For example, Marconi, the inventor of radio, was created a marquis, while D'Annunzio, of Fiume fame (page 19), received a generous pension and a palatial villa for his services to Fascism. The *Duce* used his newly created Fascist Academy to offer plum jobs and fat salaries to leading professors. Few could resist such temptations, particularly when they were well aware that any sign of dissent would lead to their immediate dismissal.

Other professions were regulated by the regime. Teachers had to join a Fascist Teachers' Association in order to keep their jobs, while musicians were required to join a National Fascist Union of Musicians. A small number did resist – the famous conductor, Toscanini, went into exile in 1929 – but the great majority joined.

The regime also used these tactics of fear and self-interest to deter opposition from the general public. Party membership became increasingly necessary for those seeking work or promotion in the public sector. Dissent could mean dismissal and

Key question
Why was there little opposition to Fascism?

persistent offenders might even be sent to some poor remote southern hill-town to serve a sentence of internal exile.

Impact of propaganda on support for Fascism

Key question
To what extent did propaganda generate support for Mussolini?

The regime was determined not only to deter opposition but also to build up popular support. Extreme propaganda was its principal weapon. This propaganda, of which the cult of the *Duce* was a very important part, stressed the genius of Mussolini, the impossibility of opposition and the supposed achievements of Fascism. Much was heard of Fascist successes in foreign policy, such as Yugoslavia's cession of Fiume to Italy (page 112). Italians were informed that foreigners were loud in their admiration for the *Duce* and his policies. They were promised that Italy under Fascist rule would regain the greatness it had known under ancient Rome and during the Renaissance. Mussolini hoped to capture the imagination of the public and to win their commitment to the transformation of Italians into an energetic, disciplined, obedient and warlike people. Parades, processions, the press and education were all used in an attempt to convey the message that the present was one of the great moments in Italian history and that Italians had a duty to participate in this adventure.

It is uncertain how many Italians were fully convinced by this incessant propaganda – probably relatively few – but it appears that the *Duce* was personally very popular. For most Italians, at least until the late 1930s, the dictator was producing stability at home and success abroad. His regime seemed to be providing moderate prosperity without intruding too far into private lives and without making excessive demands on the public, while foreign adventures, as in Ethiopia, excited patriotic interest. Given this record, there seemed to be little need for opposition and, in any case, Italians were well aware that opposition was likely to prove highly dangerous.

Concentration camps

Key question
How extensive was the use of concentration camps for opponents of Fascism?

It is significant that although the regime set up prison camps on remote, inhospitable islands such as Lipari and Lampedusa, off the Italian mainland, these were on a much smaller scale than the Nazis' concentration camps for political dissidents. While several hundred thousand opponents of the Nazis were imprisoned Italian camps probably held fewer than 5000 prisoners. Conditions were tough, and some torture did occur, but the brutality was not systematic.

Mussolini might occasionally advocate vicious punishments for those who did actively oppose him but, in practice, Italian Fascism preferred to cajole its subjects into outward conformity, rather than ruthlessly to root out potential dissenters.

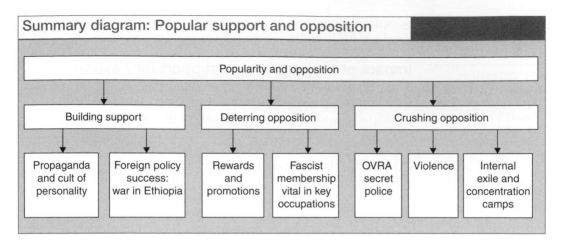

Summary diagram: Popular support and opposition

8 | Key Debate

How popular was Mussolini's Fascist regime?

Contemporary views on the popularity of the dictatorship were mixed. Many foreign journalists were impressed by the apparently spontaneous enthusiasm displayed at Fascist rallies and believed the *Duce* to be extremely popular. Italian anti-Fascist exiles, on the other hand, stressed the brutal, repressive aspects of the regime, and argued that only fear deterred widespread opposition.

In recent years historians have generally agreed that repression was not the only reason for the absence of effective opposition to Fascism, but there is still debate over the popularity of the regime. The prominent Italian historian, Renzo De Felice, has argued that Mussolini was genuinely popular, particularly in the years 1929–36 and culminating with the victory over Ethiopia (page 116), which was Mussolini's 'political masterpiece and greatest success'. The popular consensus in favour of Mussolini lasted until the ill-fated invasion of Greece in 1940 (page 135).

Alexander De Grand agrees that there was something of a consensus but doubts the extent of genuine popular enthusiasm. He argues that 'Fascism managed to develop a broad, if only passive, consensus after the elimination of any real alternative in 1925 and the integration of Catholics into the regime after 1929'. Martin Clark argues that 'the Fascist regime seemed tolerable and was even popular until 1937–8. It was careful not to alienate vested interests [such as Church and big business] … Active resistance seemed pointless'. Other historians have agreed that there was a distinct dropping off of support from the mid to late 1930s: C. Leeds claims 'During the late 1930s … people resented the increased interference in private life. They also resented the anti-Semitic laws …' (pages 100–1). The question then remains: would the regime have survived in some form had it not entered the Second World War or was it in terminal decline even before Italy joined the global conflict in 1940?

Some key books in the debate
M. Clark, *Modern Italy, 1871–1982* (Longman, 1984).
A. De Grand, *Italian Fascism: Its Origins and Development*
(University of Nebraska, 2000).
C. Leeds, *Italy under Mussolini* (Wayland, 1972).

9 | Comparison of Fascism and Nazism

Key question
What similarities are there in the rise to power of Fascism and Nazism?

In European history the years between the First and Second World Wars have often been described as the era of the Fascist dictators. The 1930s, in particular, have been seen as the heyday of European Fascism, with Italy, Germany and Spain all experiencing Fascist regimes. But what did these regimes (especially Fascism in Italy and Nazism in Germany) have in common? Did Italy provide a model for its German counterpart?

Rise of Fascism and Nazism

It is certainly true that both countries experienced the collapse of parliamentary democracy and its replacement by largely personal dictatorships. Economic problems, a weak party system, a perceived Communist threat and the existence of an **establishment** uncommitted to the notion of mass democracy combined to cripple parliamentary government. In the resulting power vacuum it was possible for radical groups espousing anti-Communist and anti-democratic opinions to grow. Mussolini and Hitler, as leaders of such groups, managed to convince their conservative establishments that their parties posed no fundamental threat and deserved a chance to try to tackle the economic and political crises. Once in power, however, the leaders of Fascism and Nazism showed that they would neither share their power nor relinquish it.

Key term

Establishment
The political, economic and military élite who traditionally held power in a country.

Nature of the dictatorships

The parallel between the Italian and German dictators is striking. They shared an all-consuming desire for supreme personal power over their respective countries. They were determined that power should be theirs alone. They would not tolerate any control from the conservative establishments that had helped them into power, nor were they prepared to be the servants of their own parties. The Fascist and Nazi parties would continue in existence, as would the great institutions of state, such as the civil service, but there could be no doubt where ultimate power lay.

They attempted to remove dissent and to build up support for their regimes by employing a mixture of repression, concession, propaganda and foreign adventure. Censorship and legalised state violence curbed opposition. Working compromises were sought with powerful interest groups, notably the army and industry. A cult of personality was consciously promoted, stressing the leader's genius, vision, benevolence and infallibility. Only the leader could restore national pride and secure the country's rightful place among the great European powers. This pre-eminent position was to be achieved, so the public was told, by a series of diplomatic coups or, if needs be, by war.

This approach was effective. Many ordinary people, particularly in Germany, were prepared to believe in the all-powerful, charismatic leader. The dictator's political style of dramatic, choreographed rallies, parades and spectacles suggested that here was an energetic alternative to dull and petty parliamentary politics. The US journalist William Shirer recorded his impressions of one of these rallies in Nazi Germany:

> I'm beginning to comprehend, I think, some of the reasons for Hitler's astounding success ... he is restoring pageantry and colour and mysticism to the drab lives of twentieth-century Germans.
>
> The hall was a sea of brightly coloured flags. Even Hitler's arrival was made dramatic. The band stopped playing. There was a hush over 30,000 people packed in the hall. Then the band struck up the Badenweiler March, a very catchy tune and used only when Hitler makes his big entries. Hitler appeared at the back of the auditorium and, followed by his aides, he strode slowly down the long centre aisle while 30,000 hands were raised in salute ... In such an atmosphere no wonder, then, that every word dropped by Hitler seemed like an inspired word from on high. Man's – or at least the German's – critical faculty is swept away at such moments and every lie pronounced is accepted as high truth itself.

Mussolini also recognised the importance of such a political style, as he explained in 1922:

> Democracy has taken 'elegance' from the lives of the people, but Fascism brings it back; that is to say, it brings back colour, force, picturesqueness, the unexpected, mysticism, and in fact all that counts in the souls of the multitude.

These new leaders could speak powerfully to ordinary people – as one Italian writer explained:

> Mussolini always knew how to speak a language that the people understood ... He had all sorts of feelers and antennae that made him grasp the trend of the popular mood and suggested to him the right attitude, the right slogan, that could bring popular passion to a frenzy.

Hitler possessed similar talents, as Otto Strasser, a one-time political opponent within the Nazi Party, attested:

> Hitler responds to the vibration of the human heart with the delicacy of a seismograph ... Adolf Hitler enters a hall. He sniffs the air. For a minute he gropes, feels his way, senses the atmosphere. Suddenly he bursts forth. His words go like an arrow to their target.

Influenced by the personal dynamism of the leaders, and grateful for the restoration of law and order and the return of apparent economic stability, it was possible to overlook the systematic attack on political freedoms and individual liberties. Believing the propaganda claim that the dictators were trying to create a better, less divided society, many citizens justified the state's intrusion into nearly every aspect of life. Work and leisure time, for both adults and young people, were increasingly controlled by the regime through such organisations as the Labour Front, Strength through Joy and the Hitler Youth in Germany, and the *Dopolavoro* and ONB in Italy. Certainly, some people objected to this increase of control by the state, but most realised that conformity was the safest course. They also realised that the new organisations could provide some material benefits, notably subsidised leisure pursuits and holidays.

Key question
What similarities were there over the importance of foreign expansion and war?

Foreign policy and war

As the 1930s progressed, both Mussolini and Hitler became increasingly obsessed by dreams of foreign expansion – the *Duce* in the Mediterranean, Balkans and North Africa, and the *Führer* in Eastern Europe and Russia. To prepare their populations for war, the dictators increased their attempts to militarise society. Through propaganda, education, youth training and re-armament, they tried to create a new kind of citizen – one who was obedient, disciplined, self-sacrificing and warlike. The dictators wanted to convince their publics that war was not something to be regretted, an admission of the failure of diplomacy, but rather was something to be welcomed. War was man's natural condition, and should be celebrated not decried. As Mussolini put it:

> War alone brings up to their highest tension all human energies and puts the stamp of nobility upon the peoples who have the courage to meet it. Fascism carries this antipacifist struggle into the lives of individuals. It is education for combat. I do not believe in perpetual peace; not only do I not believe in it but I find it depressing and a negation of all the fundamental virtues of man.

This stress on war and the attempt at the militarisation of society appealed to only a relatively small section of the population, and must have irritated or appalled many ordinary Italians and Germans. However, as long as the dictators could continue to deliver foreign policy successes at minimum cost, their popularity was assured. Mussolini's own personal popularity reached a peak in the aftermath of the Ethiopian war, while Hitler's diplomatic victories over the Rhineland, Austria and the Sudetenland brought him massive support. To the citizens of Italy and Germany their leaders were finally restoring national pride and putting an end to the frustrations and humiliations caused by the peace treaties drawn up at the end of the First World War.

Those Germans and Italians who were impressed by the easy diplomatic victories of the 1930s were less enthusiastic about the prospect of a general European war. Berlin in 1939 and Rome in 1940 experienced none of the war hysteria that had been so widespread 25 years earlier on the outbreak of the First World War. Nevertheless, such was the faith in their leaders that the public remained confident that victory would be cheap and easy. Italians were soon relieved of this illusion, but most of their German counterparts, buoyed up by the defeat of France in 1940, were to keep their faith in the *Führer* until the very last months of the war.

The war, and the war alone, brought about the destruction of the two regimes, but not before the dictators had wreaked havoc on their own peoples and on Europe. Italy was fought over by foreign armies and fell into a bitter and bloody civil war. Germany saw millions of its citizens die and witnessed the destruction of its industry and infrastructure. The country was divided into four by the victorious powers.

The influence of Italian Fascism on Nazism

Hitler admitted that he had an admiration for the *Duce* and said that the 'march on Rome' in 1922 had provided a model for his own, abortive, 'Munich *putsch*' a year later. Mussolini's use of propaganda and the promotion of a cult of personality provided Hitler with inspiration. Italian blackshirts and their violent, paramilitary methods influenced the Nazi SA, the brownshirts. Hitler may also have learned important lessons from Mussolini's courting of powerful conservative groups and the worried middle classes in the years immediately before and after 1922. The Italian regime's attempts to control its citizens' lives, via education, the ONB and the *Dopolavoro*, also provided some models for the Nazi state.

> **Key question**
> To what extent did Hitler copy the methods of Mussolini?

However, despite these examples, it is possible to exaggerate the similarities between the dictatorships. The regimes were not carbon copies of one another. As Hitler himself remarked, 'from the failure of the Munich *putsch* I learnt the lesson that each country must evolve its own type and methods of national regeneration'. The differences between the two dictatorships were significant.

Differences in the power of the Fascist and Nazi dictatorships

One notable difference between the regimes was in the degree of power the dictators could exercise over their citizens. The Nazi state compelled greater loyalty and obedience from its citizens. The regime's dramatic foreign policy successes brought Hitler a degree of popularity that the *Duce* could only envy. The *Gestapo* rooted out opposition more thoroughly than did its Italian equivalent, the OVRA. Even passive dissent was attacked. From the very beginning of the Nazi regime in 1933 the number of people finding themselves designated as political opponents

> **Key question**
> Why was the Nazi regime able to exert greater control over its citizens than its Italian counterpart?

and placed in concentration camps was much higher than in Fascist Italy.

The Nazi state intruded further into ordinary life than did its Italian counterpart. At the workplace Germans were increasingly influenced and controlled by the Nazi Labour Front, while their children were subject to indoctrination at school and pressurised into joining the Hitler Youth. Nazism even tried to attack traditional religious beliefs by setting up its own National Reich Church which hoped to replace the Cross and the Bible with a sword and a copy of *Mein Kampf*.

Mussolini, of course, also attempted to control, transform and militarise his people and employed similar methods, but he met with less success. Differences between German and Italian society help to explain why the *Duce* faced a more difficult task. The strong, authoritarian government established after unification of Germany in 1871 had demanded the loyalty of its citizens and offered social stability, a heady, nationalistic foreign policy and a fairly comprehensive system of social and welfare benefits in return. Many Germans, particularly among the upper and middle classes, eagerly supported this regime and welcomed the rapid economic growth it brought with it. Germans, then, were accustomed to a disciplined society and used to a government that stressed the importance of the military.

Furthermore, economic growth led to the development of excellent communications links within Germany and permitted a great expansion of state education. The Nazis benefited from this habit of obedience to the state and used the national media and agencies of the state, such as schools, to spread and enforce the Nazi message. In such an advanced industrialised society, it was easier to disseminate new ideas and to identify and eradicate opposition.

Italy, in contrast, possessed no such tradition of popular obedience to a strong government. The Liberal regime had struggled to impose its will on the new state and had not extended the role of government as far as its German counterpart. Italy remained a country where central government was viewed with great suspicion. Commands from Rome were often ignored, particularly in the south. Italy remained poor, despite the economic growth at the turn of the century. As a result Liberal governments were permanently short of money and were unable to fund an extension of state education properly or to improve the poor state of Italian communications. Fascist ideas could be spread with ease in the cities and towns of the more prosperous parts of northern Italy, but in large areas of the south, where illiteracy and poverty were common, the peasants remained largely ignorant of the *Duce*'s great plans for his country.

The existence within Italy of a powerful Catholic Church also limited the influence of Fascism. Mussolini's need for Catholic support forced him to hide his own anti-clericalism and to conclude a concordat guaranteeing the independence of the Church and permitting the continued existence of Catholic schools. During the 1930s, Mussolini tried to intimidate the

Church over such issues as the Catholic youth movement, but he never felt able to batter the Church into submission. For the *Duce* there was no possibility of creating a rival Fascist Church on the Nazi model.

Racial ideology

The dictatorships differed not only in the degree of power they exerted over their respective societies, but also in one crucial part of their ideology – the question of race. The *Führer*'s determination to create a 'master race' of pure Aryans decisively influenced both his domestic and foreign policies. If the master race was to come into existence then 'race defectives' must be removed and the *untermenschen* or sub-humans subjugated. Within Germany this justified the murder of thousands of the mentally and physically handicapped, and the systematic persecution of the Jews. In foreign policy this justified the racial war against the Slavs in the east and the genocide practised against the European Jews. Hitler had never disguised his anti-Semitism – *Mein Kampf* was littered with references to the Jews. By 1939 he could tell parliament:

Key question
How far did the dictators share a common racial ideology?

> If the international Jewish financiers in and outside Europe should succeed in plunging the nations into a world war, then the result will not be bolshevisation of the earth [a global Communist state] and thus the victory of Jewry, but the annihilation of the Jewish race in Europe.

Hitler took his obsession to the grave. Writing his final will and testament in 1945 he stated:

> Above all, I demand of the nation's leaders and followers scrupulous adherence to the race laws and to ruthless resistance against the world poisoners of all peoples, international Jewry.

The *Duce* did not share this obsession. Mussolini believed that Italians had an innate superiority over other peoples but he never developed a racial ideology to underpin Italian Fascism. He did introduce anti-Jewish laws in the late 1930s but this action seems to have been prompted by pressure from his new ally in foreign policy adventures, Adolf Hitler. In fact, the *Duce*'s anti-Semitism, to the extent that it genuinely existed at all, developed very late in the day. He had told one interviewer in 1932:

> Anti-Semitism does not exist in Italy. Italians of Jewish birth have shown themselves good citizens and they fought bravely in the war. Many of them occupy leading positions in the universities, the army and the banks.

The Italian racial laws caused great hardship, but, unlike their German counterparts, the vast majority of Italian Jews avoided the Nazi death camps.

The Nazi racial ideology sponsored the growth of the SS, supposedly a pure Aryan élite. Conceived as an ultra-loyal bodyguard to the *Führer*, the SS grew in power, particularly during the Second World War. It formed its own very well-equipped military units, administered large areas of the conquered territories in the east, and controlled the death camps. Italian Fascism possessed no such organisation. The blackshirt militia lacked energy and leadership. Where it did take part in military action, notably in the Spanish Civil War, it was singularly unsuccessful. Mussolini, for all his talk of the Fascist revolution, had little interest in the blackshirts once he had secured power.

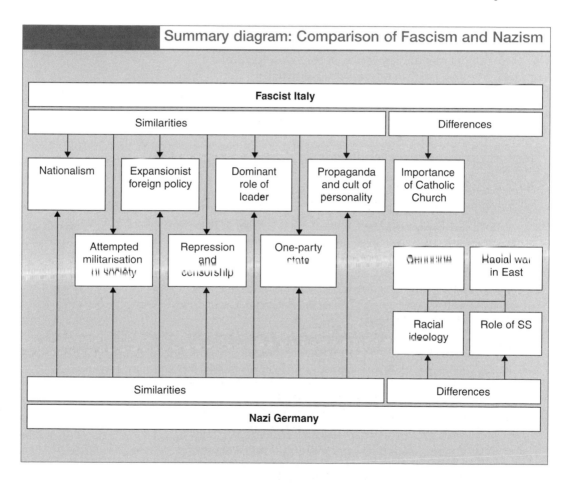

Summary diagram: Comparison of Fascism and Nazism

Study Guide: AS Questions

In the style of AQA

Read the following source and then answer the questions that follow.

Adapted from: M. Kitchen, Fascism, *1992.*

Fascists proclaimed the existence of a genuine community, based on the leadership principle.

(a) What is meant by the 'leadership principle' in relation to Fascist Italy? (3 marks)

(b) Explain why the regime in Fascist Italy promoted the role of the single leader. (7 marks)

(c) 'Propaganda was the key factor in the consolidation of the regime'. With reference to Fascist Italy (1922–39), explain why you agree or disagree with this statement. (15 marks)

Source: AQA, May 2002

Exam tips

The cross-references are intended to take you straight to the material that will help you to answer the questions.

(a) You will have little more than five minutes in the exam to answer this challenging question. Even under such time pressure it is worth jotting down a rough plan. The 'leadership principle' claimed that the *Duce* should have no limits to his power over parliament, government and the Fascist Party itself. Briefly point out:
- Mussolini's powers as dictator regarding parliament and the making of laws (page 56).
- Mussolini's control over government and the Fascist party (pages 61–5).

You should also explain briefly that there were, in reality, some constraints on this 'leadership principle' – for example, it was still possible for him to be dismissed as Prime Minister (page 137).

(b) Your answer should focus on:
- Mussolini's determination to establish personal rule (page 57).
- Fascist propaganda claiming, for example, that dictatorship meant strong, decisive government, as opposed to the constant squabbling within the coalition governments of the Liberal era (pages 57–61).
- The weak organisation of the Fascist Party which prevented the Party from taking a leading role in the formulation of policy and the choice of ministers (pages 63–5).

(c) This question clearly requires you to explain the ways in which the Fascist regime used propaganda both to generate support and to deter opposition. Your explanation should include:
- Cult of personality (pages 57–61).
- Propaganda claims of success in foreign policy (pages 57–61).

- Propaganda claims of success in economic policy (pages 57–61).
- Propaganda claims of success in social policy (pages 57–61).

The question also asks you to consider whether propaganda was the key factor in establishing and helping to maintain the dictatorship. You will have to examine the importance of other factors, principally:

- Mussolini's tactics in the period 1922–5 which enabled the creation of the dictatorship (pages 45–52).
- The use of violence and repression 1922–39 (pages 67–9).
- Mussolini's accommodation with powerful groups in Italian society (page 63).

In your answer you should weigh the importance of propaganda against these other factors. Decide what you will argue at the outset and organise your answer carefully to support your view. Your final paragraph should provide a conclusion which summarises the argument you have made.

In the style of OCR

To what extent was Mussolini able to achieve a total dictatorship by 1928? (45 marks)

Source: OCR, January 2003

Exam tips

The cross-references are intended to take you straight to the material that will help you to answer the question.

A fatal mistake would be simply to write the story of how Mussolini created his dictatorship. Instead, you must analyse what a 'total dictatorship' would mean in practice and then explain how far Mussolini had achieved each aspect of a 'total dictatorship'. The following table will give you some help in planning your answer.

Aspects of a total dictatorship	Steps taken by Mussolini towards achieving this aspect	Limits to Mussolini's power
Personal rule	The *Duce* gained right to make own laws 1926 (page 52) Control of Fascist Party (pages 63–5) Control of government (pages 61–2) Abolition of democratic elections (page 49)	Ability of King to sack Prime Minister (page 50) Remaining power of key groups in Italian society (pages 75–6)
Propaganda and cult of personality	Pages 57–61	Pages 57–61

Removal of opposition	Pages 67–70	Pages 67–70
Control of media	Pages 68–9	–
Control of leisure and social life	Pages 105–7	Pages 105–7
Control of education	Pages 102–5	Pages 102–5
Control of economy and working lives	Corporate state (pages 83–4)	Pages 83–4

Point out the links between aspects of the dictatorship; for example, the cult of personality was closely linked to the aim of personal rule, and also helped deter opposition. Lastly, don't forget that although the question requires you to consider Mussolini's actions after he became Prime Minister in 1922, you are not expected to assess the dictatorship in the 1930s: do end your analysis in 1928.

Study Guide: Advanced Level Question

In the style of Edexcel
'From 1924, Mussolini and his Fascists were in total control of the Italian state.' How far do your agree with this opinion? (60 marks)

Exam tips
The cross-references are intended to take you straight to the material that will help you to answer the question.

This question clearly asks you to explain the methods used by Mussolini to establish and maintain his dictatorship, and to evaluate the extent of their success. You should make reference to such issues as:
- The reduction of the role of parliament, establishment of personal rule, abolition of free elections (page 52).
- Control of government and civil service (pages 61–2).
- The use of violence and repression (pages 67–9).
- The use of propaganda (pages 57–61).
- Control of the media (pages 68–9).
- Control of education (pages 102–5).
- Control of leisure (pages 105–7).
- Control of the economy and working life (pages 83–4).

To consider the extent to which Mussolini had control over the Italian state you will need to point out the limits to Mussolini's control. For example, the Catholic Church remained highly influential within the state (see page 99), as did *Confindustria*, the employers' organisation (page 84).

In your conclusion, you must make an overall judgement about the extent of Fascist control, summarising your key arguments.

6

Mussolini and the Economy 1922–40

POINTS TO CONSIDER
Mussolini claimed that his economic policy would transform the organisation of the Italian economy and prepare the nation for war. This chapter examines the extent to which the *Duce* achieved his aims, focusing principally on:

- Mussolini's aims
- Impact of Fascist policies, particularly the corporate state, on Italian industry and living standards
- Impact of Fascist policies on Italian agriculture and living standards
- The extent to which Fascism transformed and modernised the Italian economy

Key dates
1925   Vidoni Palace Pact banned independent trade unions
1925   Start of Battle for Grain
1926   Abolition of right to strike
1926   Ministry of Corporations set up – start of corporate state experiment
1927   Revaluation of the lira damaged Italian economy
1929   Start of global economic depression
1936   Mussolini increased drive for economic autarky
1939   Parliament replaced by the Chamber of Fasces and Corporations

Key question
In what ways was Mussolini trying to transform the Italian economy?

1 | Mussolini's Aims

Mussolini, like Hitler, was no economist. He had little knowledge of, or interest in, the workings of the economy and on coming to power had no coherent programme. Mussolini was, however, determined to hang on to power and therefore, in his early years in office, he adopted economic policies that would make his position secure. As the 1920s progressed, Mussolini became more ambitious and increasingly attracted to the idea of an economic transformation of Italy. He proclaimed the world's first 'corporate state', supposedly a radically new way of organising and running a nation's economy, different from and superior to both the capitalist economies of Britain and the USA and the Communist economy of the USSR.

By the mid-1930s, his priorities had begun to change again. His war in Ethiopia (see pages 116–18) and his ever closer association with Nazi Germany (see pages 102–22) convinced him that a new type of economic transformation was vital. Fascist Italy would need an economy capable of building and maintaining a modern war machine. In a major war, foreign imports of raw materials or food might be cut off, crippling the war effort. Italy, Mussolini declared, must strive for **autarky** – economic self-sufficiency. Mussolini's preoccupations first with the corporate state and then with autarky meant that the country's 'old problems' – industrial underdevelopment, rural poverty, the north–south divide and illiteracy – were largely ignored. They were only tackled with any determination if they were obstacles to the achievement of the *Duce*'s principal aims.

(see pages 116–18)

(see pages 102–22)

2 | The Impact of Fascist Policies on Italian Industry

Mussolini was lucky enough to come to power just as Italian industry was beginning a period of 'boom'. The economic climate throughout Europe was improving and many Italian companies were able to sell their products abroad with ease. Indeed, exports, particularly of cars, textiles and agricultural produce, doubled in the period 1922–5.

Policies 1922–7
The new political regime claimed the credit for increasing company profits and attempted to win over the support of industrialists by appointing an economics professor, Alberto de Stefani, as Treasury Minister. De Stefani's economic policy was traditional and reassuring to industrialists because it limited government spending, which helped to fight inflation. He also reduced state intervention in industry – the telephone network was taken out of government control and handed back to private companies, while taxes levied on industries that had made huge profits from government contracts during the First World War were either reduced or abandoned. Industrialists were also pleased by the outlawing of Socialist and Catholic trade unions by the Vidoni Palace Pact of 1925 (see page 63).

Battle for the lira
However, after 1925, Mussolini began to take less notice of business interests. The dismissal of de Stefani and the **revaluation** of the Italian currency were two early but important examples of this. Revaluation was particularly significant. By 1926 the boom was coming to an end and the exchange rate of the lira was falling against other currencies. The exchange rate slipped to around 150 lira to the pound, a rate Mussolini that found unacceptable. Announcing his 'battle for the lira' he declared:

(see page 63).

Key terms

Autarky
Economic self-sufficiency allowing a country to operate without importing food or other key materials from other countries.

Revaluation
The Fascist government tried to increase the value of the lira against other countries' currencies.

Key question
What actions did Mussolini take to gain the support of industrialists?

Vidoni Palace Pact banned independent trade unions: 1925

Key date

Key question
What were the consequences of the 'battle for the lira'?

The Fascist regime is ready to make the sacrifices needed, so that our lira, which is itself a symbol of our nation, our wealth, our efforts, our strength, our sacrifices, our tears, our blood, is and will be defended.

Key dates

Abolition of right to strike: 1926

Ministry of Corporations set up – start of corporate state experiment: 1926

Revaluation of the lira damaged the Italian economy: 1927

To emphasise his point that his strong, vibrant country should have a strong, vibrant currency he decided to try to set a new rate of exchange of 90 lira to the pound in December 1927. This decision, restoring the value of the lira to its value in October 1922, the month of his accession to power, increased Mussolini's prestige both with foreign bankers and with the Italian public. Thus the *Duce*'s main aim had been achieved. But, the effects on the Italian economy were far from beneficial. At a stroke, foreign buyers found Italian goods nearly twice as expensive, and it was not surprising that Italian export industries, particularly textiles, went into depression. Unemployment trebled in the years 1926–8. Even Fiat, the huge vehicle manufacturer based in Turin, was exporting fewer cars in the late 1930s than it had done in the early 1920s.

The revaluation of the lira should have helped the Italian consumer because imports of foods and other products from abroad should have become cheaper. However, the *Duce* prevented this by placing high **tariffs** on many foreign imports. The only winners in economic terms were those industries such as steel, armaments and shipbuilding that needed large supplies of cheap tariff-free imported raw materials. It was these heavy industries that would be promoted throughout Fascist rule. They made healthy profits from the protected domestic market while export industries were neglected.

Key question
How far did the corporate state transform the Italian economy?

Corporate state – the theory

At first, the workers benefited from the economic revival of the early 1920s. Unemployment fell and de Stefani's policies curbed inflation. Admittedly, the years 1925 and 1926 saw the banning of independent trade unions and the abolition of the right to strike, but Mussolini claimed to be about to transform the Italian economy. He would create a '**corporate state**', a supposedly revolutionary method of running an economy. Corporations would be set up for each sector of industry and within each corporation there would be employers and Fascist trade unions to represent the workers. Each corporation would organise production, pay and working conditions in its own industry. If employers and Fascist trade unions could not agree then they would go to a labour court, administered by the new Ministry of Corporations, where the dispute would be sorted out quickly and amicably.

The Fascist regime claimed that this system would see employers and workers co-operating to maximise production for the good of the nation. Unlike Britain and France, there would be no bitter industrial disputes that led to strikes and class conflict. Unlike Communist Russia there would still be a role for businessmen whose energy and entrepreneurship would help industries to prosper.

Key terms

Tariffs
Taxes placed on imports of foreign products.

Corporate state
Every industry would be part of a Fascist-led corporation that would sort out disputes between workers and management, and help to organise production, pay and conditions.

Corporate state – the reality

At first it did appear that the Fascist trade unions might provide a real say for workers in the running of their industries, but rivalries within the Fascist Party, and Mussolini's reluctance to alienate big business interests, soon destroyed any such hopes. Rossoni, the head of the Fascist trade union movement, certainly envisaged a major role for his unions but he was opposed by the employers' organisation. *Confindustria* (see page 47) disliked all kinds of trade unions and was determined to ensure that businessmen kept control of their industries. In the middle was the Ministry of Corporations headed by the Fascist Giuseppe Bottai. He distrusted Rossoni, saw little role for the unions, and wanted to see corporations dominated by a partnership of employers and technical experts from his own Ministry. This, he hoped, would be the best way to maximise industrial production. All sides now looked to the *Duce* to clarify his vision of the corporate state.

In 1927 Mussolini came down on the side of Bottai and *Confindustria*: Bottai was charged with the task of writing a 'Labour Charter' setting out the rights of workers. When this charter was finally produced it posed no threat to the employers – private ownership of businesses was declared the most efficient method of running an economy and, as for workers' rights, employers might but were not obliged to provide annual paid holidays. Employers were also given the power to alter working hours and night shifts without any real consultation.

Rossoni's radical influence was reduced still further in 1928 when his single confederation of Fascist trade unions was split into six smaller federations and his followers in these federations were removed from their posts.

Three years after its creation in 1926 the Ministry of Corporations claimed success. The corporate state was ushering in a new economic era and had removed all class conflict in industry. By 1934 there were 22 corporations covering nearly every area of the economy and with the apparent ability to influence every aspect of industry. The reality, however, was quite different. Workers were unable to choose their own representatives in their corporation, and instead had Fascist nominees foisted on them. These Fascist officials tended to side with the employers' representatives over the key issues of wages and working conditions. Only on issues such as sick pay for workers and the belated introduction of paid national holidays in 1938 did the corporations further workers' interests. Industrialists, on the other hand, were allowed to keep their own non-Fascist employers' organisations, and largely ignored the very existence of these corporations. That regulations issued by corporations were only advisory meant that employers maintained their power and independence.

In truth, the 'corporative revolution' never materialised. Conflict between employer and employee was not solved, only suppressed, and the corporations never achieved the pivotal role in the state and the economy envisaged by the *Duce*. Although parliament itself was replaced by the Chamber of Fasces and

Parliament replaced by Chamber of Fasces and Corporations: 1939

Key date

Corporations in 1939, this meant nothing. Parliament had long lost any power and the new Chamber was equally impotent.

Depression

Key question
How effectively did the Fascist state deal with the depression of the 1930s?

Key term

Depression
A period of economic stagnation that began in the USA and affected all European industrialised countries for most of the 1930s.

Key date

Start of global economic depression: 1929

Following the Wall Street Crash in the USA, the early 1930s saw a global economic **depression** that Italy did not escape. A large number of companies collapsed and car production fell by 50 per cent. From under half a million in 1928, unemployment had risen to two million by 1933.

The democratic governments of Western Europe and the USA were reluctant to intervene to help the private sector out of its difficulties as their traditional economic philosophy of *laissez-faire* regarded such actions as reckless: raising the money to help struggling industries might plunge the government into serious debt. The Italian Fascist state had no such worries. It introduced public works schemes, notably the building of motorways and hydroelectric power plants, which put the unemployed back to work. This was important because it significantly increased the amount of money in circulation which, in turn, stimulated demand and created more jobs. The state also did much to avoid the banking collapse which affected the USA and Germany in particular. Banks had lent money to industry, but many companies could no longer meet the repayments on their loans. The banks therefore found themselves without enough money to pay their investors. The Fascist government simply stepped in and 'bailed out' the banks.

A result of this intervention was the creation of the Institute for Industrial Reconstruction (IRI) in January 1933. Many banks had major shareholdings in Italian companies and when these banks were 'bailed out' of their financial troubles IRI took control of these shares. The Italian state, in the guise of IRI, thus became the major shareholder and therefore the effective owner of many top Italian companies. IRI also took over from the banks the responsibility for providing loans for Italian industry. In addition it attempted to promote the latest managerial techniques, with some success.

The government's measures may have cost the taxpayer a great deal of money, but they did enable Italy to weather the depression a little better than its democratic neighbours. Indeed, Mussolini was delighted to hear his admirers claim that President Roosevelt had copied the *Duce*'s example when drawing up the US's 'New Deal'.

Preparing for war

Key question
How well prepared for war was Italian industry?

Mussolini's economic policies had never been designed simply to increase the wealth of the country or the prosperity of the ordinary Italian, and this became very apparent by the mid-1930s. As the dictator became increasingly pre-occupied with foreign affairs, living standards and the general welfare of the economy suffered. He believed that war, either in Europe or to further his African Empire, was almost inevitable and that Italy must be prepared. The armaments industries must be promoted, and Italy's economy must become self-sufficient. Italy should be an autarky – able to supply itself with all the food and material needed to fight a modern war.

The **economic sanctions** imposed by the **League of Nations** after Italy's invasion of Ethiopia in 1935 seemed to prove his point that there must be no reliance on imports. Mussolini therefore encouraged heavy industries such as steel, chemicals and shipbuilding by placing large government contracts. State control was expanded to the point where 80 per cent of shipbuilding and 50 per cent of steel production was directed by the government. Economies of scale were looked for and the regime allowed major companies to merge into near-monopoly organisations. Fiat, for instance, controlled car manufacturing, while Pirelli dominated rubber, and Montecatini chemicals. Exports, as usual, took low priority.

The limits of autarky

Despite these efforts the Italian economy was still far from self-sufficient when the *Duce* joined the Second World War in 1940: key materials such as oil, and coal and iron ore for the making of steel, still had to be imported in very large quantities. Italy was unable to match its enemies' levels of production and could not even replace its losses in shipping and aircraft. The drive for autarky in fact only succeeded in worsening Italy's financial difficulties. The government was spending huge sums on contracts related to the autarkic and closely related rearmament programme and also had to fund expensive military adventures in Ethiopia and Spain (see pages 116–21). Ever aware of the need to maintain popularity, the regime did not want to bring in major tax increases and, consequently, government expenditure greatly exceeded its income by the late 1930s. The remedy for these massive government deficits was either swingeing cuts in military expenditure or very significant reductions in living standards. Typically, Mussolini refused to recognise the seriousness of the economic situation and the problem remained unsolved when Italy entered the Second World War.

Impact of industrial policy on living standards

According to the *Duce*, under the corporate state, conflict between workers and bosses would end, and workers would no longer be 'exploited' and would gain greater prosperity and increased respect within society. Open conflict between employers and workers did indeed decline, but only because free trade unions were banned and strikes ruled illegal. As for greater prosperity, many industrial workers actually suffered a serious decline in their standards of living.

As the economic revival petered out in the late 1920s, industry responded with wage cuts. In the early 1930s some of these wage cuts were offset by falling prices in the shops, but, from the mid-1930s, prices began to rise steeply as Mussolini's drive for autarky pushed up the cost of imported goods. Overall, it is estimated that during the period 1925–38 real wages for the Italian worker

Key date
Mussolini increased drive for economic autarky: 1936

Key terms

Economic sanctions
To pressurise Italy into seeking a peaceful solution to the Ethiopian crisis, the League banned trade with Italy in certain goods such as grain, steel, and textiles. However, the ban did not include oil, the one commodity that would have damaged the Italian war effort.

League of Nations
International organisation of over 100 countries designed to help to prevent wars and end disputes between countries.

Key question
How did the industrial workers fare under Fascism?

fell by over 10 per cent. Falling consumption of meat, fruit and vegetables showed the impact of declining incomes. At the same time, unemployment began to rise, despite the public works programmes, and totalled some two million by 1933. This was a figure close to that of Britain, after allowing for the difference in populations.

The middle classes were far less likely to suffer from unemployment. The number of government employees virtually doubled to a million during the Fascist period and these people were not made redundant during the depression. Many state employees were in traditional jobs such as teaching, but the most explosive growth took place in the new Fascist organisations, principally the Ministry for Corporations, but also the *Dopolavoro* (see pages 105–6), which organised leisure activities for workers. These middle class office workers did suffer wage cuts during the 1930s but it was noticeable that these cuts were less than those for industrial workers.

That Fascism failed to produce real rises in living standards for the mass of Italian workers did not unduly concern the *Duce*. Instead, by December 1930, Mussolini was saying: 'fortunately the Italian people were not accustomed to eat much and therefore feel the privation less than others'. And, by 1936, he was arguing: 'We must rid our minds of the idea that what we have called the days of prosperity may return. We are probably moving toward a period when humanity will exist on a lower standard of living'.

Mussolini had never really been committed to raising the standard of living of ordinary Italians and viewed economic hardship as by no means a bad thing for his people. Economic hardship would create harder, tougher Italians dismissive of a soft 'bourgeois' lifestyle!

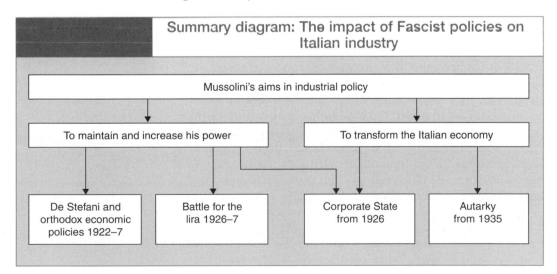

Summary diagram: The impact of Fascist policies on Italian industry

3 | Agriculture

Mussolini did not concern himself with the underlying problems of Italian agriculture – the existence of a sizeable class of poor, land-hungry peasants and the use of backward, inefficient farming methods. Instead, as with industry, he occupied himself with projects that would either increase his personal power and prestige, or supposedly help Italy to become a self-sufficient state in case of war.

The dictator's first major scheme was the '**Battle for Grain**'.

The Battle for Grain

The Battle for Grain began in 1925 and was an attempt to promote Fascist power and national self-sufficiency. Traditionally, Italy had needed to import large quantities of grain in order to feed her people. Mussolini saw this as a grave weakness, as in time of war supplies could be cut off and the country would face starvation. A campaign to increase grain production dramatically would solve this problem and would also illustrate to the world just how dynamic the new Fascist state was. Consequently, the government offered grants to enable farmers to buy tractors, fertiliser and other machinery necessary for wheat production. Free advice was made available on the latest, efficient farming techniques. Farmers were also guaranteed a high price for the grain they produced.

The incentives worked and the average harvest rose from 5.5 million tonnes per year in the early 1920s to over seven million tonnes 10 years later. Grain imports declined sharply, dropping by 75 per cent in the period 1925–35. The Battle for Grain appeared to be a resounding success and Mussolini claimed the credit. He ensured that press photographers were on hand to record him visiting farms and helping out with the harvest. Not only was the *Duce* a genius for conceiving the Battle for Grain, he was also prepared to get his hands dirty in the fields – a true leader of his people. Appearances, however, were deceptive.

The Battle for Grain certainly had dramatically increased production and helped farmers, but there had been a large price to be paid. First, much of the land in the central and southern regions that had been turned over to wheat was unsuitable for such a crop. The soil conditions and hotter, drier climate were more suited to the growing of citrus fruits or the production of wine and olive oil. The result was that these traditional agricultural exports declined.

Land reclamation

Fascism's second major initiative, and an equally highly publicised one, was land reclamation and improvement. Previous governments had made a start here, providing money to drain or irrigate farmland. Mussolini simply expanded these schemes. The Pontine marshes, only 50 kilometres from Rome, and thus easily reached by foreign journalists, were the showpiece. These malarial swamps were drained and a network of small farms was

Key question
How successful were Mussolini's agricultural policies?

Battle for Grain
Fascism's attempt to make Italy self-sufficient in the production of grain, and thus bread.

Key term

Start of the Battle for Grain: 1925

Key date

Mussolini encouraging the harvesters.

set up, owned by ex-servicemen. Overall, land reclamation was a success, since it improved public health and provided thousands of jobs during the depression. The amount of land reclaimed was, however, very limited.

Impact of agricultural policy on living standards

Key question
How did agricultural workers fare under Fascism?

Agricultural workers suffered even heavier wage cuts than industrial workers during the 1930s. In the past, a way out of this poverty had been emigration. In the first two decades of the century an average of 200,000 Italians, mainly southerners, had emigrated to the USA each year. From 1920, however, the USA decided to stop virtually all further immigration. With this escape route from rural poverty closed, more Italians left the countryside

Mussolini cutting the first sod of the new city of Aprilla on the former Pontine marshes.

for the towns and cities to find work and a better standard of living. Up to half a million people left the land in the 1920s and 1930s, while between 1921 and 1941 the population of Rome doubled. And this was despite the fact that Mussolini tried to prevent all further migration.

Mussolini's resistance to migration into the cities was the result of his proclaimed love for the countryside and his desire to 'ruralise' Italy, creating a vigorous class of prosperous peasants devoted to Fascism. However, his government did nothing to bring this about. In fact, his policies brought much more benefit to large landowners than to poor and landless peasants. Such peasants needed enough land to support their families: a law to break up big estates and to distribute them to the peasants had been introduced into parliament in 1922, but Mussolini quietly dropped the policy for fear of offending the great landowners, his political supporters.

The failure to break up the great landed estates only cemented the backwardness and poverty of the south. The gap between an industrialising north and a rural south had grown wider under the Liberal governments before the First World War, but with Fascist neglect it grew wider still. The fact that Mussolini visited the poverty stricken island of Sicily only once after 1924 perhaps indicates a recognition of his own regime's failure towards the south. That Italy still lay eighteenth in a table of European states as regards the daily calorie intake of its people, with the lowest Italian figures recorded in the south, provided statistical proof of Fascism's failure to tackle rural poverty.

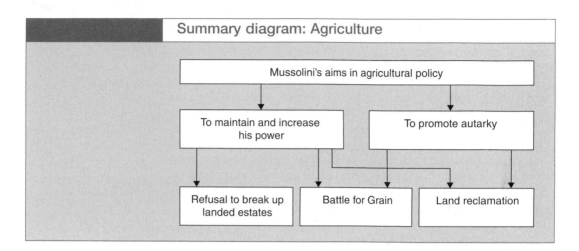

Summary diagram: Agriculture

4 | Key Debate

> How far did Fascism modernise and transform the Italian economy?

Key term

'Mussolini made the trains run on time'
This phrase was coined by foreign journalists to suggest that the Fascist regime had somehow improved the efficiency of Italian industries.

During the 1920s and 1930s many foreign journalists were impressed by Fascism's Battle for Grain, the land reclamation schemes, and the claims that the Italian economy was being modernised – summed up in the phrase '**Mussolini made the trains run on time**'. Newspapers such as the *Financial Times* were intrigued by the idea of a corporate state. Historians since the Second World War, however, have been able to peer beyond the Fascist propaganda and have been much less impressed.

A number of modern historians still argue that Fascism did much to modernise Italian industry – in the words of di Scalia, writing in *Italy, From Revolution to Republic* (1995), 'policies stimulated modern industries such as electricity, steel, engineering, chemicals … Italy's profile began to resemble that of modern European countries to a greater degree than in the past', but these historians are in a minority. Most historians do concede that some major industries such as vehicles and shipbuilding did expand and modernise, but point out that export industries and much of agriculture were neglected and stagnated. One of the most recent biographers of Mussolini, Richard Bosworth, has written 'so far as his economic policies were concerned, one Mussolinian line [policy] looked modernising, the next traditional'.

The corporate state

Historians are united in dismissing Fascist claims that the corporate state had transformed the economy and industrial relations. Alexander De Grand, a US professor of history, states that 'Fascism did not create its own unique economic system but rather grafted further statist [governmental] and bureaucratic tissue on the existing body of Italian capitalism'. Martin Blinkhorn, a British academic, adds that 'Corporativism in practice involved the thinly disguised exploitation and oppression of labour'.

There was no radical change in the ownership of industry. Although the state, via IRI, did take greater control over many companies during the 1930s, *Confindustria*, the industrialists' organisation, maintained its power and independence. It was never a hotbed of Fascism, but recognised the advantages of working with the regime. Indeed, several presidents of *Confindustria* became ministers. These industrial barons, certainly those in heavy industry and armaments, enjoyed government contracts and the freedom to form near-monopoly organisations, but resisted Party control and attempted state direction. As Tannenbaum puts it, 'Neither Mussolini's government nor the Fascist corporations were prepared to bully Fiat, Pirelli, or the Bank of Italy'.

Winners and losers

As for winners and losers under Fascism, historians agree that while major industrialists and big landowners, particularly in the north, benefited from the regime, agricultural workers fared the worst. Although some historians, such as the British historian Williamson, point to some of the positive effects of Fascism for industrial workers, such as accident and sick pay, there is a consensus that the interests of industrial workers were ignored and repressed and their living standards fell.

Overall, there was precious little transformation of the Italian economy and this was apparent at the time. As De Grand points out, 'large numbers of Italians understood (by the 1930s) that Fascism lacked any real commitment to economic change'. Nevertheless, it is important to point out that despite Fascism's failures the development of Italian industry and agriculture up to 1940 was not disastrous. Output did increase in both agriculture and industry, and big companies did well. In the field of communications, Fascism made real progress, building *autostrade* (motorways), electrifying 5000 kilometres of railway line, and improving the efficiency of the railway system. On the other hand it should be remembered that such improvements were made principally for propaganda purposes and Italy remained relatively backward compared to Germany, France and Britain. Italy's economic underdevelopment was to be cruelly exposed during the Second World War.

Some key books in the debate

M. Blinkhorn, *Mussolini and Fascist Italy* (Lancaster Pamphlets, 1984).
R.J.B. Bosworth, *Mussolini* (Hodder Headline, 2002).
A. De Grand, *Italian Fascism – Its Origins and Development* (University of Nebraska, 2000).
N. Farrell, *Mussolini: A New Life* (Weidenfeld, 2003).
S. di Scalia, *Italy from Revolution to Republic* (1995), quoted in *Fascist Italy* by J. Hite and C. Hinton (John Murray, 1998).
E. Tannenbaum, *Fascism in Italy* (Allen Lane, 1973).

Study Guide: AS Question

In the style of OCR

To what extent were Mussolini's economic policies a success in the years 1925–40?   (45 marks)

Exam tips

The cross-references are intended to take you straight to the material that will help you to answer the question.

To begin with, you need to consider the various meanings of the term 'success'. Specifically you must explain how successful Mussolini was in:

- Achieving his aim of transforming the Italian economy via the corporate state, and the battles for grain and the lira (see pages 82–8).
- Achieving autarky and thus equipping Italy adequately for war (see pages 85–6).
- Using economic policy to cement his support with big business interests, such as *Confindustria* (see page 92).
- Generating popular support via propaganda successes such as the Battle for Grain and land reclamation (see pages 88–9).
- Improving the efficiency and production capacity of Italian industry and agriculture (see pages 91–2).
- Improving the living standards of ordinary Italians (see pages 86–90).

You need to make a judgement about the success or failure of each aspect of economic policy. For example, were his policies more successful in generating propaganda victories than in tackling the economic problems of Italy? If so, explain why this was the case. Examiners will also be impressed if you can explain how policies were inter-related or even contradictory: for example, if Mussolini was to maintain support from big business he could not introduce truly radical policies regarding the corporate state. Finally, you must make an overall judgement about the success of Mussolini's policies and justify your argument.

Study Guide: Advanced Level Questions

In the style of AQA

How far did any one of the totalitarian regimes you have studied maintain control of, and achieve progress in the economy?　　　　　　　　　　　　　　　　　(20 marks)

Exam tips

The cross-references are intended to take you straight to the material that will help you to answer the question.

This question can be divided into two parts. You should first consider the extent to which Mussolini's regime 'controlled' the economy. The main issues here are:

- The extent to which the corporate state brought about Fascist control of the economy (pages 83–5).
- The extent to which the battles for grain and for the lira brought about Fascist control of the economy (pages 82–8).
- The extent to which the drive for autarky brought about Fascist control of the economy.

To reach the top level five, you will need to point out that Mussolini's attempts to gain greater control of the economy varied over time: in the early years of his regime he was anxious to do nothing to alienate business supporters, but then experimented with the corporate state from 1926. By the 1930s the momentum behind the corporate state had been lost, but once the *Duce*'s attentions turned towards the thought of war, from 1935, the drive for autarky represented a renewed attempt by the regime to exert greater control over the economy.

The second part of the question, on how far the regime achieved progress in the economy, needs analysis of the following issues:

- The extent to which Fascism modernised the economy, improving the efficiency and productive capacity of both industry and agriculture (pages 91–2).
- The extent to which Fascist policies raised the standard of living of ordinary Italians (pages 86–90).

It is essential that you include statistics to back up your arguments. You should also consider whether the degree of 'progress' varied over time: there were improvements in living standards in the early 1920s but by the 1930s there were widespread wage cuts. You might also look at economic winners and losers.

In your conclusion you should make a judgement on whether or not economic progress under Fascism exceeded Fascism's control over the economy.

In the style of Edexcel

'Mussolini's economic policies achieved nothing of value for Italy in the period 1924–39.' How far do you agree with this view? (60 marks)

Exam tips

The cross-references are intended to take you straight to the material that will help you to answer the question.

In the exam spend at least five minutes planning your answer. You will be expected to show your knowledge of Mussolini's economic policies, but just describing these policies will win few marks. It is essential that every paragraph focuses on the outcomes and achievements of Fascist policies. In particular:

- Did Mussolini's policies raise living standards (pages 86–90)?
- Did Mussolini's policies promote the growth of industry and agriculture (pages 91–2)?
- Did Mussolini address the issues of rural poverty and the south (pages 89–91)?
- Did Mussolini in any way modernise the Italian economy (pages 91–2)?

It is vital that you make an overall judgement on the claim that he 'achieved nothing of value'.

7 Life in Fascist Italy

POINTS TO CONSIDER

This chapter addresses the key question of how far Mussolini changed the lives and attitudes of Italians. His efforts to do so are studied under the following headings:

- Mussolini's aims
- Fascism and the Catholic church
- Fascism and anti-Semitism
- Fascism and women
- Fascism and youth
- Fascism and social life

The chapter concludes with a discussion of the question 'How far did Mussolini achieve his aims in domestic policy?'

Key dates

1923	Pope withdrew support for Catholic *Popolari* party
1925	Fascist leisure organisation, *Dopolavoro*, set up
1926	ONB youth organisation created
1927	Launch of Battle for Births, designed to increase Italian population
1929	Lateran Agreements ended major dispute between Italian state and the Catholic Church Teachers forced to take oath of loyalty
1931	Fascist Teachers' Association set up
1938	Anti-Jewish racial laws introduced

1 | Mussolini's Aims

Mussolini's primary aim was to adopt policies that would help to secure his position as all-powerful *Duce* of Italy, but as the 1920s progressed he also revealed a desire to transform Italian society and even the Italian character. By the 1930s, he expressed contempt for what he described as the 'bourgeois mentality' of many Italians, a mentality that stressed the importance of family, religion, local loyalties and a comfortable standard of living. Mussolini intended his new Italians to place Fascism and the nation above these traditional loyalties. They would be tough, even warlike, disciplined and obedient to their *Duce*. Fascist policies designed to create these new Italians would, however,

> **Key question**
> What was Mussolini's vision for Italian society?

begin to jeopardise Mussolini's support among both the public and powerful groups, such as the Church.

2 | Fascism and the Catholic Church

Mussolini wanted to see Fascism penetrate every aspect of Italian society, but he was neither systematic in his ideas nor prepared to force through policies that might make him unpopular. His realisation that Fascism must compromise in order to secure support was particularly evident in his dealings with the Church.

Mussolini never lost the anti-religious attitudes of his youth, but he was aware that the Catholic Church occupied an important place in the lives of millions of Italians. He recognised that an accommodation with the Catholic Church could bring him great public support and increase the prestige of his regime abroad. As early as 1921 he told the Italian parliament:

> I affirm in this House that the Latin tradition of Imperial Rome is today represented by Catholicism: I believe that, should the Vatican definitely give up its … dreams [of political power], Italy should afford the Vatican all material help and encouragement for its schools, its churches, [and] its hospitals. Because the development of Catholicism in the world, an increase in the 400 million men who look towards Rome from all parts of the earth, is of interest and a source of pride for us Italians.

By the time he became Prime Minister in 1922 Mussolini was posing as an alternative to anti-Catholic Liberals and 'godless' Communists and Socialists. Restoring Catholic education in state schools and increasing government payments to priests secured the confidence of the Pope who, in 1923, withdrew his support for the *Popolari*, the Catholic political party. These moves neutralised, at least temporarily, the Church as a potential source of opposition. However, it did not mean that Fascism had the active support of the Vatican – this would only come with the **Lateran Agreements** of 1929.

Lateran Agreements

The treaty and concordat that comprised the Lateran Agreements officially ended the conflict between Church and State that had existed since the foundation of the Italian kingdom some 60 years earlier. The Pope had resented the Italian state's seizure of his own territories of Rome and the Papal states, in central Italy. In the 1929 treaty, the Pope agreed to recognise the Italian state and its possession of Rome and the old Papal states. In return, the state recognised the Pope's control over the **Vatican City**, part of Rome but independent from the Italian state. The Pope also received financial compensation of £30 million for surrendering his claim to Rome.

The concordat established Catholicism as the state religion of Italy and outlined what this would mean in practice:

- the Pope could appoint all bishops, but the government could veto any politically suspect candidates
- the state would pay the salaries of the clergy
- clergy could not belong to political parties
- religious education, of a Catholic nature, would be compulsory in state schools
- there would be no divorce without the consent of the Church
- couples wishing to marry would no longer have to attend a civil ceremony in a register office – a Church service would now give full legal recognition to the marriage.

The Lateran Agreements signalled that Mussolini had given up any hope of removing the influence of Catholicism from Italian society. Nevertheless, he was very happy with the deal. Clerics could not become a focus of opposition and, more importantly, the Church would throw its support behind Mussolini as *Duce*.

While the Lateran Agreements were hailed as a great achievement, not all Italians were impressed. The exiled intellectual G.A. Borgese attempted to explain why the Church had reached such an accommodation with Fascism, and outlined what he saw as the consequences:

> There was no reason why Pope and *Duce* should not come together: no reason except in Christ; but Christianism was by no means the most decisive factor in Pope Ratti's mind. He was sure that he loved Italy; it is sure that he hated democracy and Socialism ... the ruthless anti-Christianity of Fascism was nothing to him.
>
> The Church became [a collaborator with] atheistic tyranny, and tyranny rewarded it by making it supreme in ... the family. Marriage and divorce became a monopoly of the Vatican, and the priest lent his hand to the [Fascist] in ... the purpose of national violence and international anarchy.

Tensions between Fascism and the Catholic Church

Key question
Why did the Lateran Agreements not end all conflict between Fascism and the Church?

Although the Lateran Agreements were hailed as a triumph by both Mussolini and the Pope, the 'love affair' between Catholicism and Fascism was not a smooth one and it cooled as Mussolini tried to shape society into a more Fascist mould.

The first open dispute between Church and State came in 1931 when the government attempted to suppress the Church-sponsored Catholic Action. This body provided a rival to Fascism's own youth and leisure organisations. A compromise was reached confining youth groups within Catholic Action to purely religious activities, but the Church remained determined to preserve its influence over the young. The Church made it clear that the Fascists must not attempt to suppress Catholic schools or interfere with the Catholic University of Milan and the Federation of Catholic University Students. The Church even had the confidence to declare the creed of the Fascist Balilla (see page 103) blasphemous. This resistance to Fascism's totalitarian claims to control every aspect of life was also shown by Radio Vatican's broadcasting of alternative news and information.

In the mid and late 1930s senior clergy did support Italian involvement in the wars in Ethiopia and Spain as they saw them as 'Christian Crusades', spreading and defending the faith, but from 1938 tensions between the regime and the Church surfaced again over the issue of anti-Semitism. As the regime brought in a raft of anti-Jewish laws (see page 100), Pope Pius XI voiced his disquiet. By 1939, the alliance between Catholicism and Fascism was over, and the Pope openly regretted the Church's earlier eagerness to embrace the *Duce*.

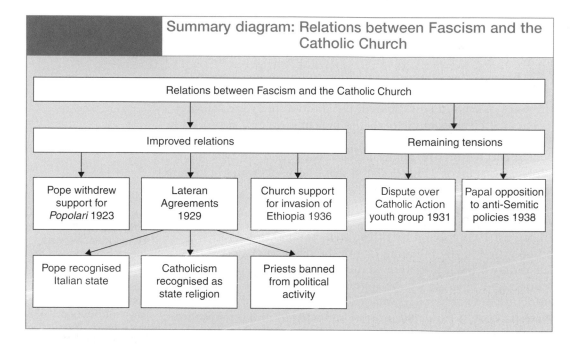

Summary diagram: Relations between Fascism and the Catholic Church

3 | Fascism and Anti-Semitism

The *Duce* had never shared Hitler's obsessive hatred of the Jews and had even had a Jewish mistress, Margherita Sarfatti. In 1932, Mussolini stated that Italian Jews 'have always behaved well as citizens and fought courageously as soldiers'. Nor was anti-Semitism prominent among leading Fascists: Italo Balbo had close ties to the Jewish community. Foreign Secretary Ciano wrote in his diary in 1937 'Nor do I believe that we should unleash in Italy an anti-Semitic campaign. The Jews are few, and, but for some exceptions, good'. The regime even allowed 3000 German Jews to enter the country as refugees from Nazi persecution. Why then did active persecution of Jews begin in 1938?

By the mid 1930s Mussolini's foreign policy goals had brought the regime closer to the Nazi regime in Germany (see pages 120–2). Nazi racial ideas now began to circulate in Italy, and Mussolini found himself persuaded that there was a Jewish influence behind resistance to Fascism both in Italy and across Europe. The *Duce* began to see significance in the fact that several members of the Italian anti-Fascist group 'Justice and Liberty' (see page 67) were Jews. French opposition to Italian involvement in the Spanish Civil War could apparently be explained by the presence of a Jew, Leon Blum, in the position of Prime Minister.

The first clear example of the influence of Nazism appeared in July 1938 when the regime gave official blessing to the claims of Italian anti-Semites by publishing a tract entitled the 'Manifesto of Racial Scientists'. This declared that 'the Jews do not belong to the Italian race'.

Anti-Semitic policies

In August 1938 foreign-born Jews were banned from state schools, and in the following month the ban was extended to Italian-born Jews. Jews were banned from teaching in state schools and separate schools were to be set up for Jewish students. In October, Jews were excluded from membership of the National Fascist Party and professional and cultural organisations, and prevented from owning large companies or large landed estates. From November 1938, they were even forbidden to marry non-Jews. Jews were also to be excluded from posts in the military and banking.

Italian Jews suffered severely under these anti-Semitic laws, losing much of their liberty and their standard of living. They lived under the constant fear that Fascism might adopt the murderous policies of their Nazi allies. Indeed, Mussolini was well aware of Nazi atrocities against Jews in Eastern Europe by 1942 yet voiced no objection to them. However, at least until 1943, the regime did not collaborate with Nazi plans to exterminate all Jews in Europe. In fact, implementation of Italy's anti-Jewish laws was inconsistent.

The anti-Semitic laws contained exemptions for those Italian Jews who had served in the First World War or who had served the Fascist regime in some capacity. Farinacci, for example, kept

Key question
Why did Mussolini pursue anti-Semitic policies?

Key question
How extensive was the persecution of the Jews?

Key date

Anti-Jewish racial laws introduced: 1938

his Jewish secretary. In addition, many government and Fascist officials made little effort to enforce the laws, either because they shared the Church's view that persecution was wrong, or because they had personal or family connections with Jewish Italians. Mussolini's own sons protected their Jewish friends from harassment.

If persecution was not nearly as systematic as in Nazi Germany, there was a hard core of racist Fascists who advocated the full-scale adoption of Nazi genocidal policies. The same Farinacci who had kept his Jewish secretary asserted, said in 1942, 'The Jews want to destroy us; we will destroy them'. When the original Fascist regime collapsed in July 1943 and was replaced by the Italian Social Republic (see pages 139–40) Mussolini allowed these racist Fascists their head. A decree of November 1943 ordered the confiscation of Jewish property and the rounding up of all Jews. Over 7500 Italian Jews were sent to Nazi death camps in Eastern Europe. Only 600 survived.

4 | Fascism and Women

Key question
What was Fascism's policy regarding the role of women?

One sphere of life where Fascist policy and Catholic belief coincided was the role of the sexes. Catholicism held that birth control and abortion were unnatural and offensive to God, which implied that woman's role should be that of wife and mother. Fascism shared this traditional attitude towards the place of women and was happy to ban contraception and to encourage women to have children. Schools emphasised traditional gender roles and the regime tried to discourage girls from entering higher education. However, the *Duce*'s concern was not simply to confine women to a domestic role – he wanted to raise the population dramatically and so provide soldiers for his armies and colonists for the new Italian Empire.

Battle for Births

Key question
How successful was the Battle for Births?

Key date
Launch of Battle for Births, designed to increase the Italian population: 1927

The 'Battle for Births', launched in 1927, was designed to increase the population from 40 million to 60 million by 1950. Mussolini specified 12 children per family as the ideal. To achieve this, a series of 'carrot and stick' measures was introduced. Marriage loans were offered to encourage couples to have more children. Part of the loan repayment was cancelled as each new child was born. A further financial inducement was that a married man with at least six children was exempt from all taxation. In addition, health care for mothers and infants was improved. Propaganda suggested that all good Italians had a duty to produce children for the *Duce*. Indeed, Mussolini gave prizes to the most prolific mothers.

For those still reluctant to become parents, penalties were introduced. Bachelors were taxed increasingly, to the point where the government raised some 230 million lira in 1939, and, by the late 1930s, jobs and promotions in the civil service were open only to the fertile married.

Pressure was exerted on women to stay at home: private companies promoted married men, and the state railway company sacked all women who had been appointed since 1915, with the exception of war widows. In 1933 a quota system was introduced into the public sector, limiting women to 10 per cent of the workforce. In 1938 this was extended to large- and medium-sized private firms. Of course, the quota system was not applied to traditionally female, low-paid occupations such as cleaner or waitress! Such discrimination revealed Fascist prejudices and was designed to help to win the Battle for Births. But it also proved useful in coping with the unemployment problem.

Despite all the measures, and to Mussolini's mystification, the Battle for Births was lost. The rate of marriage remained unchanged, while the birth rate declined until 1936 and rose only slightly thereafter. Indeed, the 1936 figure of 102 live births per 1000 women of child-bearing age compared very unfavourably with the 147 per 1000 in 1911. As for the target population of 60 million by 1950, all the *Duce*'s efforts could only produce 47.5 million Italians by this date. During the Second World War Mussolini reflected bitterly that Italians' lack of patriotic effort in this field had lost him the equivalent of 15 army divisions. Even in the workplace, Fascist policies towards women had only limited success. Despite all the pressure to exclude them from paid employment, women still made up 33 per cent of the industrial workforce in 1936, a fall of only three per cent since 1921.

5 | Fascism and Youth

Mussolini's dream of millions of aggressive, athletic, disciplined Fascists spreading Italian power overseas led to his interest in the education and training of the young. He was also fully aware that loyal youth could help to preserve the regime both at the time and in the future.

Key question
How did Mussolini attempt to ensure that Fascist ideas were adopted by the young?

Schools

If Mussolini was to influence the youth of Italy he needed to ensure that schools promoted Fascism. The regime took measures to compel the loyalty of teachers: teachers of suspect political views could be dismissed from 1925, and from 1929 all teachers were required to take an oath of loyalty to the regime. In 1931 a Fascist Teachers' Association was set up to regulate the profession, and membership was compulsory by 1937.

In schools the cult of personality was heavily promoted. Teachers were ordered to stress Mussolini's genius and were supplied with sycophantic biographies for use in the classroom. The *Duce*'s portrait had to be hung alongside that of the King. Italian youth was to have absolute, unquestioning faith, as the compulsory textbook for eight-year-olds explained:

Key dates
Teachers' oath of loyalty: 1929

Fascist Teachers' Association set up: 1931

The eyes of the *Duce* are on every one of you. A child who, even while not refusing to obey, asks 'Why?' is like a bayonet made of

milk. You must obey because you must. What is the duty of a
child? Obedience! The second? Obedience! The third? Obedience!

Mussolini had, apparently, been sent by providence to restore
Italian greatness and students must learn to take pride in the
Italian nation. Accordingly, history and Italian literature became
priorities in schools. Existing books that were insufficiently
patriotic were banned. In 1926 this amounted to 101 out of 317
history texts in schools and, by 1936, a single official text was
compulsory. Students were to be left in no doubt that Italy had
been the cradle of European civilisation and that Italians had
always been at the forefront of events. After all, Marco Polo had
been Italian, as had Michelangelo and Christopher Columbus.
According to the Fascists it had been Italian victories in the First
World War that had saved Britain, France and the USA from
defeat! Above all, under the guidance of the *Duce*, Italy would be
restored to her rightful place in the world, as the creed of the
Fascist youth organisation made clear:

> I believe in Rome the Eternal, the mother of my country, and in Italy
> her eldest daughter, who was born in her virginal bosom by the
> grace of God; who suffered through the barbarian invasions, was
> crucified and buried, who descended to the grave and was raised
> from the dead in the nineteenth century, who ascended into heaven
> in her glory in 1918 and 1922. I believe in the genius of Mussolini,
> in our Holy Father Fascism, in the communion of its martyrs, in the
> conversion of Italians, and in the resurrection of the Empire.

Young people were to identify themselves with Mussolini, Fascism
and Italy and to see the three as inseparable. To build a new Italy,

A typical propaganda stunt to reinforce the cult of personality: Italian children form the name of
their *Duce*.

young people had to work together and see themselves as a group. Mussolini outlined this in 1932:

> Here in Italy we educate them in accordance with the ideal of the nation, whereas in Russia children are brought up in accordance with the ideals of a class. Still, the ultimate aim is identical. Both in Italy and in Russia the individual is subordinate to the state.

Fascist youth movement

Fascism was not just concerned with what happened at school, but also determined to influence young people in their leisure time. The *Opera Nazionale Balilla* (ONB) was set up in 1926 to organise youth movements and, by the early 1930s, membership had become compulsory at state schools for all children from the age of eight. By 1937, over seven million had joined the ONB. The Fascist propagandist Missiroli explained its aims, organisation and activities:

> It is a moral entity having as its objectives the assistance and moral and physical education of the youth of the country carried out by means of a continuous activity inside and outside the schools and intended to transform the Italian nation 'body and soul'. The Opera performs its functions through the *Balilla* and *Avanguardisti* institutions. Children from 8 to 14 years old belong to the *Balilla*

Fascist youth movement, the ONB, set up: 1926

Key date

Members of the *Balilla* Fascist youth greet Mussolini. What does the photograph suggest were the principal aims of Fascist policy towards the young?

and the *Avanguardisti* include boys from 14 to 18 years of age. In respect of girls, the *Piccole Italiane* correspond to the Balilla, and the *Giovani Italiane* to the *Avanguardisti*.

ONB activities focused largely on military training and Fascist ideology, but also included sport and fitness training. There were regular parades and annual summer camps. Girls were also involved in some sport and ideological training, but activities such as sewing, singing and child care betrayed the traditional role Fascism expected of women.

At university level there was the youth organisation, GUF (*Gruppi Universitari Fascisti*), which promoted Fascist ideas, and further sporting and military training.

Key question
What was the purpose of the *Dopolavoro*?

Key date
Fascist leisure organisation, *Dopolavoro*, set up: 1925

6 | Fascism and Social Life

Dopolavoro

Despite all these efforts, Mussolini was not content to wait for youth to grow up and transform the Italian character. He sought to influence adult Italians there and then. Ordinary Italians had been tamed at work, through the banning of trade unions and by other Fascist controls, and the regime tried to maintain this control outside the workplace. The *Dopolavoro* was set up in 1925 to provide leisure activities that would influence workers towards a Fascist view of life and compensate for the now defunct trade-union-sponsored clubs.

The *Dopolavoro* organisation expanded quickly and by the mid-1930s controlled:

- all soccer clubs
- 1350 theatres
- 2000 drama societies
- 3000 brass bands
- 8000 libraries.

Virtually every town and village, even in the south, had its *Dopolavoro* clubhouse and membership had risen from 300,000 in 1926 to 2.4 million in 1935, representing 20 per cent of the industrial workforce and 7 per cent of the peasantry. Membership peaked in 1939 at four million.

Coercing people into membership was rarely necessary as working class Italians were quick to take advantage of subsidised sports, entertainments, excursions and holidays. The *Dopolavoro*'s popularity was also due to the fact that only lip service was paid to Fascist ideas of physical and military training. The emphasis was not on indoctrination, but on having a good time. The relative absence of propaganda can be illustrated by the programme of the theatre company *Carro di Tespi*. Of the seven plays performed in Rome in 1938, five were comedies or farces, and only two were serious plays, neither of which had any direct relevance to Fascist ideology.

Increasing Fascist interference in social life

If the *Dopolavoro* was a popular initiative, other Fascist policies affecting ordinary people only lost support for the regime. The late 1930s saw the attempted introduction of a range of initiatives which Mussolini believed would shake Italians out of their smug 'bourgeois mentality' and make them take a more vigorous, Fascist approach to life. However, his directives proved counter-productive, appearing to most Italians as petty, interfering and ridiculous. For example, the Fascist salute, a replacement for the handshake, was officially made compulsory in 1937, while in the following year Italians were told to stop using *'lei'*, the polite form of address, and instead say *'voi'*, a word apparently more completely 'Italian' in derivation. Attempts were made to change the calendar so that Year 1 would be 1922, the year of the Fascist seizure of power.

Even fashion was subject to the whims of the *Duce*. Fascism condemned women for wearing make up and even tried to ban them from wearing trousers. Such rules were unenforceable and simply irritated Italians.

Key question
How successful were Fascist attempts to alter the behaviour of ordinary Italians?

7 | How Far Did Mussolini Achieve His Aims in Domestic Policy?

The *Duce*'s principal aim was to maintain and increase his power, and his domestic policies did bring him substantial public support. Mussolini was constantly portrayed as an infallible genius, a man, even a superman, destined to lead Italy back to greatness. The *Duce*, so it was said, had a brilliant, original mind, but also appreciated the thoughts and needs of ordinary Italians, a claim emphasised by press photos of him helping out in the harvest (page 89) and laying the foundations of some new building or *autostrada*. Fascist initiatives were apparently always great successes, while Fascist failures such as the Battle for Births were quietly forgotten.

Italians were not wholly taken in by this incessant stream of propaganda, but they were not averse to the *Duce*'s claims that Italy possessed the greatest civilisation. They enjoyed Italian successes, such as victories in the 1934 and 1938 soccer World Cup and Primo Carnera's winning of the World Heavyweight Boxing Championship. The *Duce*, of course, claimed the credit. However, much of Mussolini's enhanced support derived from the apparent results of foreign policy. In fact, his concordat with the Catholic Church was perhaps his only real achievement of any note in the domestic sphere and even that was beginning to sour by the late 1930s.

Mussolini had hoped to transform the Italian character and Italian society into a Fascist mould, but he was disappointed. The race of athletic, aggressive, obedient, Fascists never materialised. Fascism did not penetrate the psyche of most Italians, changing traditional habits and attitudes. There was outward conformity but little inner conviction. Although Fascist propaganda claimed that it was transforming Italy, the reality was rather different.

Fascism might claim, for example, to be creating a Fascist youth via control of the school curriculum and the power of the ONB, but it is uncertain how many true converts there were. A substantial proportion left school at the age of 11 and so avoided the full programme of indoctrination, while in private and Catholic schools the state curriculum and ONB membership were never enforced. Even those who experienced a full Fascist education and progressed to university may not have been convinced: in 1931 the head of Fascist organisation for university students admitted that 'the masses in the universities are not yet what the *Duce* wants ... those furthest from us are students of law, literature and philosophy ...'.

Parents and the older generation were still more resistant to change, as they showed by their 'unpatriotic' reaction to the Battle for Births, and by their irritation at being told to adopt the new Fascist salute, the new form of address and the instructions on what to wear. Fascist policies might be welcomed if they afforded some apparent advantage, such as *Dopolavoro* cheap holidays, but were resisted if they seemed to threaten entrenched customs and habits. Thus in the late 1930s, as Fascism tried to intrude further into everyday life, popular support for the regime began to decline. Furthermore, the Fascist government had neither the means nor the self-confidence to force through unpopular policies.

Mussolini had brought stability of a sort to Italy. He remained in power for 21 years, being personally popular for the greater part of this time, but he had not brought about a revolution.

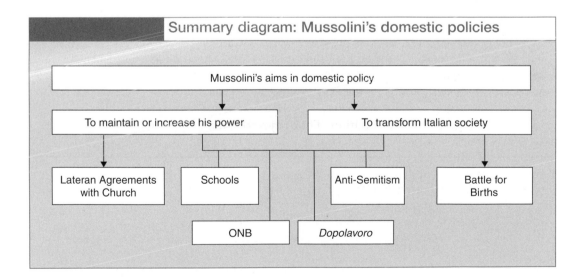

Summary diagram: Mussolini's domestic policies

Study Guide: AS Questions

In the style of OCR

To what extent were Mussolini's social policies a success during
the period 1925–40?   (45 marks)

Exam tips

The cross-references are intended to take you straight to the material that will help you to answer the question.

A useful approach is to draw up a table or grid to help you to organise your thoughts.

Area of social policy	Mussolini's aims in this area	Successes	Failures	Mark out of 10
Relations with Church	Pages 97–9	Pages 97–9	Page 99	
Women and Battle for Births	Pages 101–2	Pages 101–2	Page 102	
Youth	Pages 102–5	Pages 102–5	Page 107	
Social life	Pages 105–6	Pages 105–6	Pages 106–7	
Anti-Semitism	Pages 100–1	Pages 100–1	Pages 100–1	

You can use the final column to make your overall assessment about the extent of Mussolini's success in each area. Seven or eight out of ten would indicate that you thought the *Duce* had achieved most of his aims in that policy area.

Once you have completed the planning grid and awarded your marks, you can then work out the structure of your answer. Do write an opening paragraph setting out Mussolini's overall aims, and then explain those areas where he was more successful. Don't write 'I give him seven out of ten' – instead, say something like 'Mussolini did have significant success in his relations with the Church …'. Once you have explained those areas where Mussolini did have some success, move on to an examination of those areas where Mussolini was less successful. Try to analyse why he was less successful with some policies – were there any common factors?

Don't forget your conclusion where you will make your judgement about Mussolini's overall success or failure.

Study Guide: A2 Question

In the style of Edexcel

'Mussolini's hold on Italy in the years 1924–39 owed more to the success of his domestic policies than to his use of terror.' How far do you agree with this view? (60 marks)

Exam tips

The cross-references are intended to take you straight to the material that will help you to answer the questions.

It is important to remember that this question expects you to consider not just Mussolini's social policies and his use of terror (pages 67–9 in Chapter 5), but also his economic policies as addressed in Chapter 6. In fact your assessment of Fascist economic policies will make up a significant part of your answer.

You can use the subheadings in Chapters 5–7 to help you to plan your answer. Your plan will need to address the following issues:

- To what extent was the relative absence of opposition the result of Mussolini's use of terror (pages 67–70)?
- To what extent was the relative absence of opposition the result of propaganda and censorship (pages 57–61)?
- To what extent was the relative absence of opposition the result of successful domestic policies such as the Lateran Agreements (pages 97–8) and *Dopolovoro* (pages 105–6)?
- To what extent was the relative absence of opposition due to successful economic policies – were living standards improving (pages 86–9)?

Before writing your answer, you will need to decide on the relative importance of each factor. If, for example, you judge that terror was *not* the most important factor then you should start your answer with a discussion of the role of terror. You can conclude this section with a linking statement to the main body of your answer, perhaps along the lines of: 'Terror certainly helped deter opposition but more significant was …'.

8 Mussolini's Foreign Policy 1922–40

POINTS TO CONSIDER

Foreign policy was a key concern for Mussolini. He intended to make Italy a great power, an equal to Britain and France in Europe, and with a dominant position in the Mediterranean. He would expand the Italian Empire in Africa and his foreign policy successes would strengthen the Fascist position at home.

This chapter examines Mussolini's attempts to achieve all this, through the following headings:

- Mussolini's aims
- Diplomacy 1922–32
- German–Italian relations 1933–5
- War in Ethiopia 1935
- Alliance with Germany 1936–9
- Entry into the Second World War

Key dates

1923		Corfu incident used by Mussolini to promote Italian power and prestige
1924		Pact of Rome – Yugoslavia ceded Fiume to Italy
1925		Locarno Treaties – Mussolini posed as a major European statesman
1926		Treaty of Friendship increased Italian influence over Albania
1933		Hitler came to power in Germany
1933–4		Conflict over Austria
1935		Italian invasion of Ethiopia
1936	September	Italian troops sent to Spain to aid 'Fascists' in civil war
	November	Rome–Berlin Axis formed – Mussolini drew closer to Nazi Germany
1939	April	Italian invasion of Albania
1939	May	Pact of Steel with Germany committed Italy to the Nazi side in a future European conflict
1939	September	Germany's invasion of Poland started the Second World War
1940	May	German invasion of France
	June	Italy entered the Second World War on the Nazi side

1 | Mussolini's Aims

Key question
What did Mussolini mean when he said he wanted to make Italy 'great, respected and feared'?

On coming to power in 1922, Mussolini did not have any clear foreign policy. It was apparent that he had completely rejected the **anti-imperialist**, anti-war beliefs of his youth, but it was uncertain how far he had adopted the views of his political allies, the nationalists. He had loudly supported entry into the First World War and had condemned the peace settlement – the 'mutilated victory' (see page 19) – but it was unclear what revisions to the peace treaties he would seek.

There was no foreign policy 'master plan', but in his first few months in office the new Prime Minister did begin to develop a general aim – in his words, 'to make Italy great, respected and feared'. Italy would achieve great-power status via military build-up, diplomatic intrigue and, if need be, war. Italy would one day be the dominant power in the Mediterranean, would develop and even expand its colonial empire in Africa, and would have the **Balkans** as its own **sphere of influence**. The *Duce* would be the architect of all this, and would have transformed the Italians into a more energetic and aggressive people in the process.

However, until the 1930s these plans lacked detail. Mussolini was not sure which colonies would expand. Nor did he know how he would achieve 'dominance' in the Mediterranean, or how much power he desired in the Balkans. Nevertheless, the *Duce*'s overall objectives remained the same, even if circumstances, particularly the general situation in Europe, would force him to adopt a variety of tactics in pursuing these objectives.

The *Duce* soon recognised that foreign affairs could provide him with the ideal stage – he would impress his fellow-countrymen with spectacles where he would overshadow foreign statesmen, and defend and promote Italian interests with unending success. He would conduct foreign policy himself, avoiding the old, stuffy foreign office, and reap international prestige and internal support. Foreign affairs came to take up more and more of his time.

Mussolini appears to have convinced himself that he was beginning a new era in Italian foreign policy. In truth, desire for great-power status, high military expenditure and colonial adventures had also been a feature of the Liberal regime. However, Mussolini exceeded his Liberal predecessors in his ambitions and pursued his goals more relentlessly and recklessly, particularly in the 1930s. He squandered vast sums on colonial conflicts, and led Italy into a disastrous world war, the result of which was the collapse of Fascism, the onset of civil war and the death of the *Duce* himself.

Key terms

Anti-imperialist
Opposition to expanding Italy's empire.

Balkans
Area of south-eastern Europe including Greece, Albania and Yugoslavia.

Sphere of influence
An area where Italy would be the dominant power.

2 | Diplomacy 1922–32

Italy in 1922 had a secure position in Europe but was unable to exert a great deal of influence, either diplomatically or militarily. The potential threat to its northern frontiers had been removed by the friendship with France and the dismemberment of the Austro-Hungarian Empire, and Italy had no powerful enemies. However, it was Britain and France that were the dominant powers of Europe. They were the enforcers of the Versailles settlement, their colonies dominated Africa and their fleets controlled the Mediterranean. Furthermore, France was busy consolidating its political and economic influence in Central and Eastern Europe, including the Balkans. Any changes in the European **status quo** would require the consent of Britain and France, and smaller powers had few means of extracting concessions. A resurgent Italy would have to move carefully. Mussolini was to learn this lesson in his first real foray into European affairs.

Policy towards the Balkans
Greece and Corfu

In August 1923, an Italian general and four of his staff were assassinated in Greece. They had been working for the international boundary commission set up under the terms of the peace settlement and were advising on the precise location of the new Greek–Albanian border. On hearing of the assassinations, Mussolini blamed the Greek government and demanded a full apology together with 50 million lira in compensation. When the Greeks refused, he ordered the bombardment and occupation of the island of Corfu, off the Greek mainland (see the map on page 124). The European powers, led by Britain and backed by its Mediterranean fleet, demanded that Italy withdraw. The *Duce* had little choice but to agree and, although he did receive the 50 million lira compensation, he did not receive a full apology from the Greeks.

The episode was hailed in Italy as a great success for dynamic Fascism, but it also showed that, although Mussolini might be able to bully smaller powers, he was unable to stand up to the great powers. This realisation rankled with Mussolini but it made him aware of the necessity of good relations with Britain, at least in the short term. He was fortunate that Austen Chamberlain, Britain's Foreign Secretary for much of the 1920s, was an admirer of the fledgling Italian regime and was inclined to look tolerantly on the *Duce*'s actions.

Yugoslavia and Albania

Fascism had more success in the Balkans in 1924 when, in the Pact of Rome, Italy received Fiume, an Italian-speaking town on the Yugoslavian coast. This town had long been a target of Italian territorial ambitions, and had been occupied, temporarily, by Italian Nationalists in 1919 (see pages 19–20). Mussolini's

Key question
What factors limited Fascist foreign policy in the 1920s?

Status quo
The current or existing situation.

Key term

Key question
How did foreign policy successes strengthen the Fascist regime?

Corfu incident used to promote Fascist power and prestige: 1923

Pact of Rome – Yugoslavia ceded the city of Fiume to Italy: 1924

Key dates

diplomatic success therefore brought him great prestige and popularity.

The *Duce*'s success over Fiume persuaded him that Yugoslavia could be pushed around. Mussolini resented French influence in Yugoslavia and was keen to demonstrate to this new state, which had been formed only in 1919, that Italy was the dominant power in the region. He wanted to make it clear that he could make life very difficult for Yugoslavia if it tried to resist Italian influence. An opportunity to illustrate this arose in 1924 when an Italian-sponsored local chieftain, Ahmed Zog, managed to take power in Albania on Yugoslavia's southern border. The Fascist government supplied Zog with money, encouraged Italian companies to invest in the Albanian economy, and employed Italian officers as advisers to the Albanian army. By the time a Treaty of Friendship was signed in 1926 Albania was little more than an Italian **satellite state**.

Italy was clearly a potential military threat to Yugoslavia, a threat emphasised by Mussolini's funding of those ethnic minorities, notably the Croats, who wanted to break away from the Yugoslav state. Yugoslavia responded by doing its best not to antagonise Fascist Italy, but it also refused to be intimidated into subservience. Throughout the 1930s the *Duce* maintained his aggressive posture and eventually occupied much of Yugoslavia during the Second World War, after that country's defeat at the hands of Nazi Germany, Italy's ally (see map on page 124).

Relations with Britain and France

While the *Duce* was meddling in the Balkans, he was careful not to antagonise the two dominant European powers of the 1920s, Britain and France. Mussolini recognised that the main British and French interests lay in Western Europe and here he was determined to play the part of a moderate statesman. Italy remained in the League of Nations, signed the Locarno Treaties, which confirmed the permanence of Germany's western borders, and entered into the Kellogg–Briand Pact of 1928, outlawing war.

Italy and Britain also came to an agreement over the location of the border between their North African colonial territories, Libya and Egypt. However, Mussolini had little interest in the details of such treaties and pacts, and rarely took the time to read them through thoroughly. But he did see the advantages of participating in these diplomatic spectacles. He enjoyed being taken seriously as a European statesman, hoped that his apparent moderation would lead to concessions of some sort from Britain and France, and, perhaps above all, saw an opportunity to enhance his prestige and power at home. He organised dramatic entrances to international conferences, as when he raced across Lake Maggiore in a flotilla of speedboats to Locarno. Italian press coverage was always extensive, suggesting that the *Duce* was being treated as an equal by the leaders of the great powers and that Mussolini's presence and contributions had been crucial in reaching such momentous European agreements. This was gross exaggeration – at Locarno, for instance, he attended only one session of the conference and

Key term

Satellite state
A country that is very heavily influenced or virtually controlled by another state.

Key dates

Treaty of Friendship increased Italian influence over Albania: 1926

Locarno Treaties: these agreements between the European powers enabled Mussolini to pose as a major European statesman: 1925

did not even bother to read the final draft of the treaties – but it created a powerful impression in Italy.

Increasing ambitions

Mussolini posed as a good neighbour for the eyes of Britain and France but, by the late 1920s, he was increasingly determined to revise the peace settlement and make Italy 'great, respected and feared'. However, in order to do this he needed friends and stronger armed forces.

Italy signed a friendship treaty in 1927 with Hungary, another **revisionist** state, and Mussolini funded right-wing groups in Germany in the hope that a pro-Fascist government might come to power there. He even went so far as to train German military pilots in Italy, a clear breach of the Treaty of Versailles. As for military power, the dictator told the Italian parliament in 1927 that he would create an airforce 'large enough to blot out the sun'. And when he signed the Kellogg–Briand Pact of 1928 outlawing war, he immediately dismissed it in a speech to that same parliament. By the early 1930s, the Fascist regime was clearly ready to do more than meddle in Balkan affairs; it was now prepared to challenge the European status quo directly in pursuit of a 'greater' Italy. The 1930s were to see Italy becoming increasingly aggressive not only in the Balkans but in Western Europe and Africa too. What had prompted this development?

It can be argued that the regime adopted a more aggressive policy in an attempt to distract public attention away from problems at home. Mussolini certainly recognised that foreign successes would bolster his regime and, perhaps, felt that he needed new, dramatic successes now that domestic policies, such as the corporate state (see pages 83–5), were producing disappointing results, but his aims had always been expansionist and aggressive, even if circumstances had caused him to disguise this. Fascist foreign policy became increasingly belligerent, partly as the result of frustration with the limited gains won by Italian diplomacy in the 1920s, but mainly due to the recognition that the rise to power of the Nazis had transformed the European situation and opened the way for Italian ambitions. For a fuller discussion of historians' views see the Key Debate on pages 128–9.

Key question
Why did Fascist policy become more ambitious and aggressive from the late 1920s?

Revisionist
A state that wanted to change the peace treaties signed after the First World War.

Key term

Summary diagram: Diplomacy 1922–32

Aim: 'To make Italy great, respected and feared'

Peaceful diplomacy → Locarno Treaties 1925 · Kellogg–Briand Pact 1928

Aggressive diplomacy → Corfu · Albania · Yugoslavia

Key question
Why did the rise of
Hitler's Germany
encourage Mussolini
to be more
aggressive?

Key dates

Hitler came to power
in Germany: 1933

Conflict over Austria:
1933–4

Key term

Anschluss
Union between
Germany and
Austria, which had
been prohibited by
the Treaty of
Versailles.

3 | German–Italian Relations 1933–5

Mussolini realised in the 1920s that a strong, resurgent Germany, seeking revision of Versailles, would frighten Britain and France and make them more amenable to Italian demands. Indeed, neither wanted Italy as an enemy and it would, therefore, be able to play off the two camps against each other to its own advantage. Mussolini had probably funded the Nazis, along with a number of other right-wing groups, in the Germany of the late 1920s. On the face of it, therefore, he should have been delighted about Hitler's accession to power in 1933. But, in fact, early relations between the two regimes were rather difficult.

Mussolini enjoyed claiming that 'his creation', Fascism, was spreading through Europe, but he was a little apprehensive lest Germany be seen as the centre of Fascism and he be overshadowed by the new *Führer*. A more concrete concern was that this new German regime might take over Austria, thus creating a powerful 'greater Germany' that would share an Alpine frontier with Italy. If this were to occur, Italy would have lost the security of its northern border guaranteed by victory over Austria-Hungary in 1918, and might even be pressured into ceding those German-speaking areas in north-eastern Italy gained at the peace conference.

The danger of an Austro-German union (*Anschluss*) was even more apparent to the Austrian government in Vienna. Any union of the two countries would not be a merger, it would effectively be the takeover of the weaker (Austria) by the stronger (Germany). Consequently, Dollfuss, the Austrian Chancellor, looked for outside support and he visited Rome three times during 1933. He was relieved to be told that he should suppress the Nazi Party in Austria and that Italy would protect Austria from any German aggression.

In February 1934, Mussolini encouraged Dollfuss to set up a right-wing authoritarian regime which would be partly modelled on Italian Fascism, but which would be anti-Nazi. The Chancellor attempted to do this but was assassinated by Nazi sympathisers in July 1934. Mussolini was outraged and immediately despatched troops to the Austrian border to deter Germany from attempting an armed *Anschluss*. Relations between the two Fascist regimes had not got off to an auspicious start. Indeed, in 1933 Mussolini had described his fellow dictator as:

> an ideologue who talks more than he governs ... a muddle-headed fellow; his brain is stuffed with philosophical and political tags that are utterly incoherent.

On hearing of Dollfuss' assassination the *Duce* went further and called Hitler a 'horrible sexual degenerate'.

Stresa Front 1935

Relations reached a low in March 1935 when Nazi Germany revealed that it had developed an airforce, the *Luftwaffe*, in breach of Versailles and announced that it was introducing military conscription to create an army five times the size permitted by the peace treaty. In the face of this challenge, Mussolini agreed to meet the British and French in the Italian town of Stresa to organise a joint response to the apparent German threat. The result was a declaration that the three powers in the 'Stresa Front' would collaborate to prevent any further breaches in the treaties that might threaten peace.

Nevertheless, although Mussolini certainly feared and distrusted Nazi Germany, he realised that Britain and France had just as much, if not more reason, to fear Hitler. A rearmed and hostile Germany reminded the Western allies of the horrors of the First World War. The *Duce* was shrewd enough to make use of this. The 'Stresa Front' gave him added protection against an *Anschluss*, but it also indicated to him that the Western powers were anxious to avoid Germany allying with other states to revise the peace settlement. Mussolini was convinced that the thought of a German–Italian friendship would horrify Britain and France. To avoid such a possibility they might be more sympathetic towards Italian ambitions and more tolerant towards Italian adventures overseas. Mussolini saw this an ideal opportunity to expand his colonial empire at minimal risk. His chosen area for expansion was to be Ethiopia.

4 | War in Ethiopia 1935

Mussolini's aims

Key question
What was the impact of the war on Mussolini's foreign policy?

Italian invasion of Ethiopia: 1935

Key date

The *Duce* believed that Italian colonies should be developed and expanded, not for commercial motives such as to secure markets or to extract raw materials, but because a growing empire would enhance Italy's claim to be a great power. Colonies were also part of Italy's historic destiny. After all, Italy was the descendant of the Roman Empire that had controlled huge areas of North Africa and had dominated the Mediterranean. The possession of new African territories would provide another benefit: large numbers of colonial troops to enhance Italy's military might. Furthermore, an adventure in Africa offered the prospect of securing military glory on the cheap, impressing the great powers and propping up the regime's prestige at home. With the corporate state a disappointment, and the battles for grain and births (see pages 88 and 101) losing momentum Mussolini needed a new adventure to capture the public imagination.

Ethiopia was an ideal target for Mussolini's ambitions (see map on page 124). It was a large country uncolonised by Europeans, but it lacked the means to fight a modern war. The neighbouring Italian colonies of Eritrea and Somaliland provided convenient avenues of attack, while the uncertain location of Ethiopia's borders with these colonies might provide 'incidents' between the two countries' armed forces that could be used as a justification for war. Furthermore, a successful conquest would avenge Italy's humiliating defeat by Ethiopia in 1896. This, of course, would lend enormous prestige to the Fascist regime at home, proving the *Duce*'s claim that he, and he alone, could restore Italy to international grandeur.

The pretext for war

The Fascist government had taken an interest in Ethiopia since the early 1920s. Italy had sponsored Ethiopia's membership of the League of Nations in 1923 and had even signed a Treaty of Friendship in 1928. Despite these acts of a supposed 'good neighbour', the Fascist regime was, by 1929, drawing up plans to **annex** the country. In fact, in that year, Italian soldiers began to occupy disputed border areas. It was in one of these areas that, in December 1934, the incident occurred that gave the *Duce* an excuse for war. At the oasis of Wal-Wal a skirmish took place between Italian and Ethiopian troops, in which 30 Italian soldiers were killed. Mussolini immediately demanded a full apology and hefty compensation. The Ethiopian government replied by requesting a League of Nations investigation. The League agreed and set up an inquiry.

Mussolini had no interest in waiting for the results of such an investigation, as he had already issued a secret order for the 'total conquest of Ethiopia' in December 1934, and was intent on building up his military forces in the area. A huge army, together with civilian support, totalling half a million men, was transported to Africa. The announcement of German military conscription and rearmament did cause the *Duce* to pause to consider whether he was leaving himself exposed in Europe, but the Stresa conference assured him that he had nothing to fear. In addition, his conviction that Britain and France were too preoccupied with Germany to oppose him seemed to be confirmed. Talks with their Foreign Ministers during the first half of 1935 showed that both countries were prepared to accede to Italian control of at least part of Ethiopia. Britain might well object to a full conquest, but its protests would be confined to disapproving notes sent by British diplomats.

Military victory

In October 1935 Italian armies attacked Ethiopia. On the previous day the Duce had justified his invasion to the Italian public:

> It is not only our army that marches to its objective, 44 million Italians march with that army, all united and alert. Let others try to commit the blackest injustice, taking away Italy's place in the sun. When, in 1915, Italy united her fate with the Allies [in the First World War], how many promises were made? To fight the common victory Italy brought her supreme contribution of 670,000 dead, 480,000 disabled and more than one million wounded. When we went to the table of that odious peace they gave us only the crumbs of the colonial booty [in the peace treaties].

The Ethiopian forces were disorganised and armed with antiquated weapons. They were soon forced onto the defensive and suffered the full effects of modern war. The Italians used

---

Key term

Annex
Take over or seize a country.

aerial bombing and poison gas in their campaigns. In April 1936 the Ethiopian army was heavily defeated at Lake Ashangi and, in the following month, the capital, Addis Ababa, was occupied. The Ethiopian Emperor, Haile Selassie, fled to Britain and organised opposition ceased. However, sporadic guerrilla attacks continued and the Italian forces began a ruthless campaign of suppression that Mussolini was keen to encourage. He sent the following telegrams to his commander in the field:

> 5 June 1936 – All rebels made prisoner are to be shot.
> Secret – 8 June 1936. To finish off rebels as at Ancober use gas.
> Secret – 8 July 1936. I repeat my authorisation to initiate and systematically conduct policy of terror and extermination against rebels and populations in complicity with them. Without the law of ten eyes for one we cannot heal this wound in good time. Acknowledge.
> 21 February 1937 – Agreed that male population of Goggetti over 18 years of age is to be shot and village destroyed.
> 21 February 1937 – No persons arrested are to be released without my order. All civilians and clerics in any way suspect are to be shot without delay.

These brutal tactics did succeed in pacifying Ethiopia, but they did nothing to reconcile the people to Fascist rule.

'The man who took the lid off'. A David Low cartoon from the *Evening Standard*. What does the cartoonist see as the significance of Mussolini's invasion of Ethiopia? David Low, Evening Standard 4th October 1935/Centre for the Study of Cartoons and Caricature, University of Kent.

Key question
How far did the war
increase domestic
support for
Mussolini?

Italian public opinion

As the war began the mood of the public was uncertain. Some Italians, no doubt, had been taken in by the orchestrated press campaign stressing Italy's right to an East African empire and suggesting the presence of enormous quantities of valuable resources, such as precious metals, in Ethiopia, but many remained unenthusiastic. It was the condemnation of the invasion by the League of Nations that caused the public to rally round the regime in order to defend the honour of Italy. When the war was won quickly and with only around 1000 Italian casualties, Mussolini's popularity soared. The Fascist philosopher Giovanni Gentile claimed that 'Mussolini today has not just founded empire in Ethiopia. He has made something more. He has created a new Italy'. For Gentile and for many Italians, Italy was now indisputably a great power – it had proven military strength and a sizeable colonial empire, and demanded to be considered an equal to Britain and France.

Key question
Why did the war
damage relations with
Britain and France?

Impact of the war on relations with Britain and France

Public opinion in Britain and France was outraged by the invasion and the Italian tactics such as the use of gas. There was widespread support for the League of Nations' imposition of economic sanctions – no arms were to be sold to Italy and member nations were to ban the import of Italian goods. However, these measures were little more than symbolic: there was no ban imposed on the strategic commodities of oil, coal and steel and the Suez Canal (see the map on page 124) was not closed to Italian ships. Had Britain chosen to close this canal, Italy's vital supply route to its forces in East Africa would have been cut off.

These sanctions irritated Mussolini without hindering his war effort. He was convinced that Britain and France, the leading powers in the League, were timid and weak. His opinion was confirmed by the Western powers' reluctance to use the forces at their disposal and by their efforts to bring the conflict to an end by diplomatic means, culminating in the ill-fated **Hoare–Laval Pact** of December 1935. This agreement between the Foreign Ministers of Britain and France would have handed over the greater part of Ethiopia to Italy, leaving the Emperor Haile Selassie with only a small, unviable independent state. A public outcry in Britain and France put paid to this agreement, but it appeared to the *Duce* that the governments of both countries were desperate to avoid having Fascist Italy as an enemy.

Mussolini despised such apparent weakness. He increasingly saw the Western democracies as cowardly. The 1933 Oxford University Union debate in which the supposed cream of British youth had argued that they were no longer prepared to 'fight for King and Country' had probably encouraged such a notion. Mussolini thought that Britain and France were decadent, interested only in money-making and a comfortable life. His Fascism was, in contrast, dynamic and contemptuous of material

Key term

Hoare–Laval Pact
An Anglo-French
attempt to find a
compromise peace,
giving Mussolini
most of Ethiopia.

comforts. It might even replace 'bourgeois democracy' as the dominant force in Europe.

Mussolini remained willing to negotiate with Britain and France if he could see some advantage, but relations never fully recovered.

5 | Alliance with Germany 1936–9

Key question
Why did Mussolini ally with Nazi Germany?

Mussolini now looked towards Nazi Germany with more favour – here was another vibrant Fascist regime, one which had played no part in the sanctions and which, like Italy, had grievances against Britain and France dating back to the 1919 peace conferences. Mussolini thought that Italian friendship, and the prospect of a military alliance, with Nazi Germany would terrify Britain and France and would allow him to prise concessions out of them. He was still not sure exactly what these concessions might be, but he could now see the possibility of realising his dream of Mediterranean domination.

Rome–Berlin Axis 1936

A reconciliation between the two Fascist regimes had begun as early as January 1936 when Hitler agreed not to carry out an *Anschluss* and, in return, Mussolini dropped his objection to Nazi interference in Austrian politics. Europe became aware of the warming of relations when Ciano, Italy's Foreign Minister, visited Berlin in October and in the following month Mussolini proclaimed the existence of the 'Rome–Berlin Axis'. This public declaration of friendship was cemented by a secret understanding that Italy would direct its expansionist energies towards the Mediterranean while Germany looked towards Eastern Europe and the Baltic, thus ensuring that they did not compete with one another. Hitler even went so far as to suggest that he was preparing his country to be at war in three years' time.

Rome–Berlin Axis: November 1936

Key date

Hitler's talk of war did not frighten Mussolini. In fact, he revelled in such bellicose phrases and saw war as the 'supreme test' both of the individual and of the nation. Italy was rearming and, although he certainly had not committed himself to taking the country into a European war, he was prepared to risk such a conflict in pursuit of his foreign policy goals.

Intervention in the Spanish Civil War 1936

Key question
Why did Mussolini commit Italian troops to the Spanish Civil War?

From 1936 the accommodation with Germany was the central fact of Italian foreign policy. German and Italian forces fought on the same side in the Spanish Civil War that had begun in July 1936. They supported the attempts of Spanish conservatives and Fascists to overthrow the elected Republican government. Mussolini had been reluctant to get involved, at first lending only transport planes to the rebels. However, when two of these planes crashed in French-controlled Morocco, Mussolini's involvement was heavily criticised in the French press. Angry at the French reaction and determined to maintain Italian prestige, the *Duce* decided to help ensure a 'Fascist victory' in Spain. Without any

Italy sent troops into the Spanish Civil War: September 1936

Key date

real planning or thought for the political and economic consequences, Mussolini committed over 40,000 troops. Officially these were volunteers but it soon became apparent that regular Italian army units were involved. Italian troops were withdrawn only in 1939 after Republican resistance had collapsed. It had been the anti-Republican Spanish who had borne the brunt of the fighting, but the conflict had still cost 4000 Italian lives and the expenditure of over eight billion lira. It had also done nothing to improve relations with Britain and France, both of whom remained neutral during the war.

Closer Italo-German relations 1937–8

Key question
How did the *Anschluss* affect relations between Italy and Nazi Germany?

In November 1937 the 'Rome–Berlin Axis' was further strengthened when Italy joined Germany and Japan in the Anti-Comintern Pact. In practice, this was a declaration that the three countries would work together against Soviet Russia. However, the relationship between the two European Fascist states cooled somewhat in March 1938 when Hitler finally carried out the *Anschluss* without consulting the *Duce*. In response, Mussolini signed an agreement with Britain guaranteeing the status quo in the Mediterranean. But the two dictators were soon reconciled. The *Duce* had no interest in maintaining the status quo and, despite his annoyance at not being informed about the *Anschluss*, his admiration for German dynamism only increased.

Mussolini and Hitler in Munich, 1937.

In September 1938 Hitler's demands over the **Sudetenland** seemed likely to lead to a general European war. The British Prime Minister, Neville Chamberlain, asked Mussolini to act as a mediator at the conference, which had been called at Munich, to seek a diplomatic solution to the crisis. Mussolini enjoyed the favourable publicity he received in the British and French press, but he was not even-handed as mediator. In fact, he secretly colluded with Hitler to find a compromise favourable to Nazi claims. The Sudetenland was handed over to the Third Reich.

Territorial demands 1938–9

The *Duce* was hailed in Europe as an architect of peace. But, in his view, Munich had only confirmed the weakness of Britain and France, a weakness on which he was determined to capitalise. In November 1938 the Italian parliament was recalled and Mussolini instructed it to demand the annexation of Nice, Corsica and Tunis from France. In the same month he told the Grand Council of Fascism:

> I announce to you the immediate goals of fascist dynamism ... Albania will become Italian. I cannot tell you how or when. But it will come to pass. Then, for the requirements of our security in this Mediterranean that still confines us, we need Tunis and Corsica. The [French] frontier must move to the [river] Var ... All this is a programme. I cannot lay down a fixed timetable. I merely indicate the route along which we shall march.

Key question
What were Mussolini's territorial demands in Europe and Africa?

Sudetenland
The area of Czechoslovakia with a substantial German-speaking population. Hitler used this as a pretext to wage war against the Western European powers.

Key term

Mussolini taking centre stage at the Munich conference in 1938.

At last Mussolini was beginning to clarify those vague expansionist ideas that he had held for well over a decade.

By 1939, with France rearming and French opinion outraged by Italian territorial claims, the *Duce* was very aware that if he was to realise his ambitions war was almost inevitable. However, he hoped and believed that he could win a war with France, particularly if he had a military alliance with Germany. As for Britain, he had seen Prime Minister Chamberlain's desperation to avoid war at Munich and believed it would keep out of such a conflict. In February 1939 the dictator presented his most candid analysis of his foreign policy aims and made it clear that he was even prepared for confrontation with Britain, if need be. He told the Grand Council,

> Italy ... is bathed by a landlocked sea [the Mediterranean] that communicates with the oceans through the Suez Canal, ... [which is] easily blocked ..., and through the straits of Gibraltar, dominated by the cannons of Great Britain.
>
> Italy therefore does not have free connection with the oceans. Italy is therefore in truth a prisoner of the Mediterranean, and the more populous and prosperous Italy becomes, the more its imprisonment will gall [frustrate].
>
> The bars of this prison are Corsica, Tunis, Malta, Cyprus ... [all occupied by France or Britain]. The sentinels of this prison are Gibraltar and Suez [controlled by Britain]. From this situation ... one can draw the following conclusions:
>
> 1. The task of Italian policy, which ... does not have ... territorial [ambitions in mainland Europe] ... except for Albania, is to first of all break the bars of the prison.
>
> 2. Once the bars are broken, Italy's policy can have only one watchword = to march to the ocean. Which ocean? The Indian Ocean, joining Libya with Ethiopia through the Sudan, or the Atlantic, through French North Africa. In either case, we will find ourselves confronted with Anglo-French opposition.

That this was not mere bravado was shown by his instructions that detailed plans be drawn up to invade and formally annex Albania, thus intimidating Yugoslavia and making the Adriatic virtually an 'Italian sea'.

While preparations were going ahead for this invasion Mussolini received a second shock from his German friends. German troops marched into Czechoslovakia in March 1939. Again, as over the *Anschluss*, he was furious and again contemplated changing sides. Such thoughts of a major switch in policy lasted no longer than similar ideas a year earlier. Real fear of Germany was now added to grudging admiration for its successes. The Nazi state seemed intent on redrawing the map of Europe and Mussolini was convinced it had the military resources to achieve this even against the combined armies of Britain and France. Surely it was better to be friends with such a dynamic regime and pick up some of the spoils of victory?

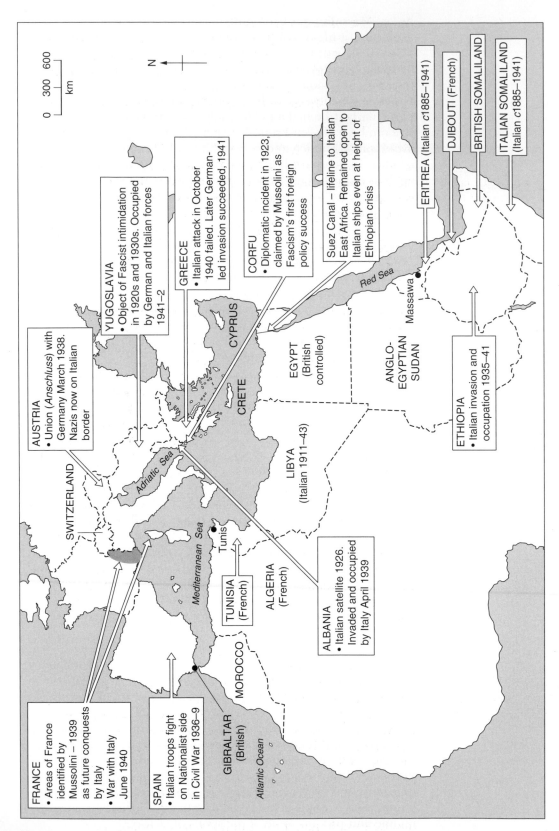

FRANCE
• Areas of France identified by Mussolini – 1939 as future conquests by Italy
• War with Italy June 1940

SPAIN
• Italian troops fight on Nationalist side in Civil War 1936–9

AUSTRIA
• Union (*Anschluss*) with Germany March 1938. Nazis now on Italian border

YUGOSLAVIA
• Object of Fascist intimidation in 1920s and 1930s. Occupied by German and Italian forces 1941–2

GREECE
• Italian attack in October 1940 failed. Later German-led invasion succeeded, 1941

CORFU
• Diplomatic incident in 1923, claimed by Mussolini as Fascism's first foreign policy success

Suez Canal – lifeline to Italian East Africa. Remained open to Italian ships even at height of Ethiopian crisis

ERITREA (Italian *c*1885–1941)

DJIBOUTI (French)

BRITISH SOMALILAND

ITALIAN SOMALILAND (Italian *c*1885–1941)

ETHIOPIA
• Italian invasion and occupation 1935–41

ALBANIA
• Italian satellite 1926. Invaded and occupied by Italy April 1939

TUNISIA (French)

ALGERIA (French)

MOROCCO

GIBRALTAR (British)

SWITZERLAND

Adriatic Sea

CYPRUS

CRETE

Red Sea

Massawa

EGYPT (British controlled)

ANGLO-EGYPTIAN SUDAN

LIBYA (Italian 1911–43)

Mediterranean Sea

Tunis

Atlantic Ocean

N

0   300   600
km

Fascist foreign policy in the Mediterranean and Africa 1922–43.

Invasion of Albania 1939

The Italian invasion of Albania finally took place in April 1939 and put the *Duce* back in the limelight. Fascist Italy was also realising its destiny by taking over weaker and 'inferior' states. The Italian regime conveniently ignored the fact that Albania had been a satellite for over 10 years. Victory was won without any major fighting.

Pact of Steel 1939

Key question
Why did Mussolini sign a military alliance with Germany?

If Mussolini was delighted with his success, he was angry that his Albanian adventure had caused Britain and France to give guarantees of military assistance to Greece and Turkey should they, too, be attacked. To the *Duce* these guarantees were an aggressive move against legitimate Italian interests: he had long considered Greece as within Italy's sphere of influence and had been trying to emphasise this point in 1923 when he had bombarded Corfu.

These guarantees may have finally convinced Mussolini to conclude a military alliance with Germany but, in any case, such an alliance was the logical conclusion of Italian actions since Ethiopia. The 'Pact of Steel' was signed in May 1939. It committed each nation to join the other in war even if that other country had caused the war by an act of aggression. In short, if Germany were to provoke a war with Britain and France, Italy would be duty-bound to enter the war on Germany's side.

It is uncertain why Mussolini agreed to such terms. Indeed, it has been suggested that he took no notice of the precise wording of treaties, regarding them as simply pieces of paper that could be discarded whenever it suited him to do so. Whether or not Mussolini understood the full consequences of the agreement when he signed it, his government soon realised its meaning and took fright. Ciano, the Foreign Secretary, seems to have persuaded his *Duce* that Italy should make its position clear to its German ally. Consequently, at the end of May the Fascist government told the Germans that, although there was no doubt about Italy's willingness to go to war, any war should be postponed for at least three years to allow it to rearm fully. An angry Hitler ignored this appeal, and did not even bother to reply.

Key dates
Invasion of Albania: April 1939

Pact of Steel, military alliance with Germany: May 1939

Nazi invasion of Poland started the Second World War: September 1939

Non-belligerence

Key question
Why did Italy not join the Second World War in September 1939?

Despite his misgivings, Mussolini made no attempt to delay Hitler's preparations for the invasion of Poland. Only at the end of August, when the attack was imminent, did he repeat his assertion that Italy needed several more years of peace. Hitler again ignored this and demanded that Italy stand by the terms of the 'Pact of Steel'. Mussolini realised that Italy was not yet in a position to fight, that such a war would be unpopular in Italy, and that the war would not be fought for Italian interests. He therefore attempted to wriggle out of his obligations by arguing that Italy would join the war only if it was supplied with enormous, and unrealistic, quantities of war material. When Germany and the Western democracies went to war over Poland in September, the *Duce* declared that his ally had been 'treacherous' and had thereby made the Pact defunct. It was then announced that Italy would be a 'non-belligerent'. The overwhelming majority of Italians were greatly relieved.

Summary diagram: The state of Italian foreign relations

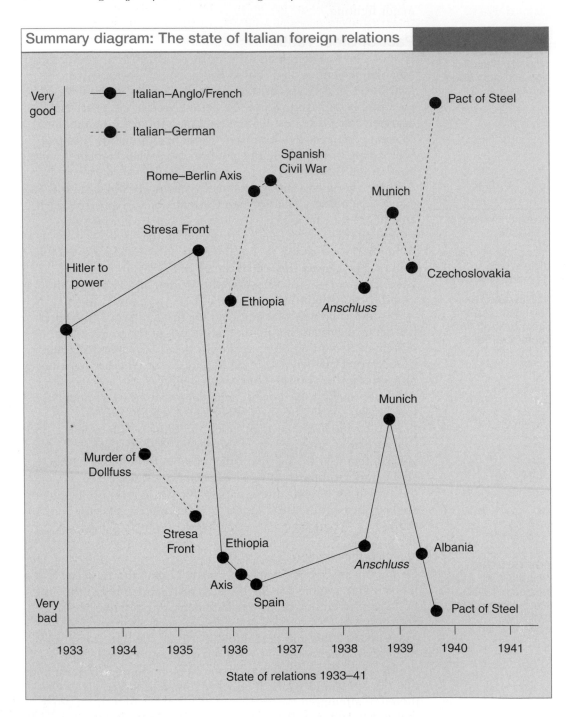

Key question
Why did Italy join the Second World War in June 1940?

6 | Entry into the Second World War

Mussolini was embarrassed by Italy's neutrality. It made him look rather pathetic after all his bellicose talk. However, he realised that the risks of intervention, both for his country and consequently for his regime, were too great. Throughout the winter of 1939 the supposedly dynamic, decisive *Duce* could not make up his mind what policy to pursue. He still favoured Germany, but was also jealous of Nazi successes and, at one point, even considered acting as a mediator to bring the sides to the negotiating table.

Key dates
Nazi invasion of France: May 1940

Italy entered the second World War on the Nazi side: June 1940

On 10 May 1940, Hitler launched his ***Blitzkrieg*** against France and the low countries, catching the Allied forces by surprise and throwing them into disarray. The Netherlands surrendered within five days and within another week the German armies had reached the Channel coast. Belgium surrendered and, by the end of May, the British Expeditionary Force had left the continent after a desperate evacuation from Dunkirk. German forces were sweeping through France and were meeting only disorganised opposition.

It appeared to Mussolini, and indeed to the watching world, that the Western allies were on the brink of total defeat. France would almost certainly collapse within days and Britain, left to fight the war alone, would probably follow within a few months or else seek a humiliating negotiated peace. The view from Rome was that if Italy remained neutral it would be faced with a Europe dominated by Germany, a Germany angry at Italy's refusal to honour its treaty obligations. Italy would have gained nothing, would lack great power status, and would be under physical threat from its Nazi neighbour. On the other hand, if Italy now committed itself to the Axis cause, Germany would be a friend and not a potential enemy. Italy and Germany would share Europe, with the Italians possibly having a free hand in the Mediterranean. In June 1940 Mussolini, therefore, decided to seize what he thought was the opportunity to redeem his lost honour and to win military glory. He declared war on Britain and France.

Key term
Blitzkrieg
'Lightning war' tactics employed by Nazis very successfully in the early years of the Second World War. Involved co-ordinated use of aircraft, tanks, and infantry.

7 | How Successful was Mussolini's Foreign Policy?

From a Fascist perspective, Mussolini could certainly claim some successes by 1940: the empire in Africa had been expanded, Albania had been seized, a pro-Fascist regime had taken control in Spain, and Britain and France had accorded Italy some respect as a great power. Foreign policy, particularly the war in Ethiopia, had also generated greater domestic support for the regime.

On the other hand, Mussolini's foreign policy goals had been far too ambitious. It was wholly unrealistic to imagine an Italy simultaneously dominating the Mediterranean militarily, expanding its colonial empire, and exercising economic and even political control over the Balkans. To have achieved even one of these aims Italy would have required far-sighted leadership, efficient and modernised armed forces, a committed populace and, above all, an advanced industrialised economy geared for war. The Fascist state possessed none of these assets.

The events of the 1920s and early 1930s had proved that Italy was not strong enough to prise major concessions from Britain and France by diplomatic means. Italy had established political control over Albania, appeared to be Austria's protector against a German-imposed *Anschluss*, and had played a highly publicised part in international conferences, but this was far from being 'great, respected and feared'.

Certainly, Hitler's rise to power did make Britain and France more tolerant towards Italian ambitions, but Mussolini was unable to adopt the role of the 'balancing power', able to exact concessions from both sides. The Western democracies would have preferred Mussolini as an ally or, more probably, as a moderating influence on the Nazi dictator, but Fascist Italy's aggressive behaviour in Ethiopia and the Spanish Civil War seemed to indicate that the *Duce* had little interest in keeping the peace. The Western powers continued to deal with Mussolini, hoping that he might restrain his Nazi friend, but by the end of 1938 they had learned to expect very little from him. It was clear to them that he was temperamentally disposed towards Germany and that whatever his territorial demands were, they were impossible to concede.

As for Germany, Hitler preferred Italy as an ally but did not take it seriously as a military power. Italian neutrality or hostility would not have deflected the *Führer* from his foreign policy goals. Indeed, both the *Anschluss* and the seizure of Czechoslovakia showed an insensitivity towards Italian interests, and when Germany went to war against Britain and France in September 1939, the Nazis were neither altogether surprised nor overly concerned by Mussolini's 'non-belligerence'.

Diplomatic methods had not succeeded in realising the *Duce*'s ambitions and the events of 1940–3 were to prove that war could not lead to the permanent expansion of the Fascist state. In fact, it would cause its destruction. Admittedly, in June 1940 Italy did appear to be in an advantageous position, with France on the brink of defeat and Britain severely weakened. However, Italy's armed forces and economy were ill prepared for a major war, as the following chapter will explain.

8 | Key Debate

How similar were the foreign policies of Fascist Italy and Nazi Germany?

Many historians have seen similarities between Fascist foreign policy and traditional Liberal policy pre-1922 – the desire for great power status, influence in the Balkans and Mediterranean and the drive for empire in Africa. Richard Bosworth, for example, sees strong parallels between Mussolini's war in

Ethiopia and the Liberal war in Libya just prior to the First World War. Bosworth argues that Mussolini's 'empire in Africa was of the old-fashioned, ramshackle, costly variety, familiar from the nineteenth century, and very different from the racial [empire] Hitler ... [wanted] ... to construct in the East on the ashes of the USSR and European Jewry'.

Bosworth raises here the controversial issue of how close Fascist foreign policy was to that of Nazi Germany. Renzo de Felice, a very prominent Italian historian, argues strongly that the two policies had little in common, and Fascist actions did not contain the racial obsession that drove Hitler into a genocidal war in Eastern Europe. Macgregor Knox, however, identifies an 'Italo-German revolutionary alliance against the west': the relationship with Nazi Germany was not just a tool for prising diplomatic concessions out of Britain and France; it was a recognition of a shared ideology, and war was its inevitable and welcomed outcome. Knox cites Fascism's brutality in Ethiopia, its adoption of Nazi racial ideas, and its aggressive territorial demands as evidence.

Bosworth, and the British historian Denis Mack Smith, have argued that neither of the two interpretations is completely accurate. Certainly, Fascist territorial demands by 1939–40 were increasingly extreme and racial policies were adopted, but Mussolini was too inconsistent to pursue a deliberate policy aimed at securing a German alliance and a general European war. For example, the *Duce* was prepared to listen to British suggestions about how to improve relations in 1937, and was non-committal towards German proposals for a military alliance in 1938. His own Foreign Secretary, Ciano, was far from supportive of the German alliance when it was signed in 1939, and the vast majority of Fascist leaders, including Mussolini himself, did not want to join the Second World War in September 1939. Neither a Fascist ideological crusade nor a skilful manipulation of the international situation for Italian advantage, Mussolini's foreign policy was characterised by uncertainty, inconsistency, opportunism and blundering.

Some key books in the debate

R.J.B. Bosworth, *Mussolini* (Arnold, 2002).
Nicholas Farrell, *Mussolini: A New Life* (Phoenix, 2004).
Macgregor Knox, *Mussolini Unleashed* (Cambridge University Press, 1982).

Summary diagram: Foreign policy in the 1930s

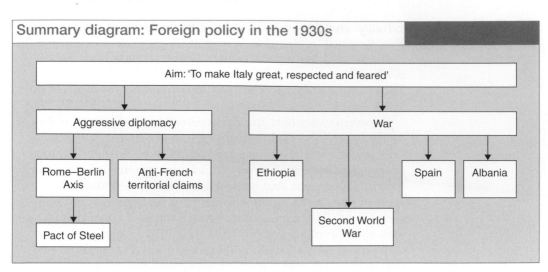

Study Guide: AS Question

In the style of OCR

To what extent was Mussolini's foreign policy a success during the period 1922–40? (45 marks)

> **Exam tips**
>
> *The cross-references are intended to take you straight to the material that will help you to answer the question.*
>
> First, you must explain what Mussolini's aims were in foreign policy (page 111). You must then assess the extent to which he achieved each of those goals. Your answer should address the following issues:
>
> - The extent to which Italy expanded its empire (pages 116–19).
> - The extent to which Italy achieved a dominant role in the Balkans and Mediterranean (pages 123).
> - The extent to which Italy became a great military power (pages 125–8).
> - The extent to which Italy became a diplomatic great power, accorded equal status by Britain and France (pages 125–8).
> - The extent to which foreign policy generated support for Mussolini within Italy (pages 112, 113, 119 and 127).
>
> Explicitly link every paragraph back to the title by commenting on the extent of Mussolini's success in each area of policy, such as the expansion of empire.
>   In your conclusion you must identify those areas in which Mussolini achieved greatest and least success, and explain the reasons for this.

Study Guide: Advanced Level Questions

In the style of AQA

To what extent were economic and foreign policies
inter-related in Mussolini's Italy? (20 marks)

Exam tips

*The cross-references are intended to take you straight to the material
that will help you to answer the question.*

In the case of Fascist Italy your answer will need to refer to the
following:

- Mussolini's use of the corporate state and the Battle for Grain to
  gain international prestige for his regime (pages 83, 85 and 88).
- The war in Ethiopia which helped raise support for the regime at
  a time when Italy was just recovering from economic depression
  (pages 116–19).
- The drive for autarky to prepare the Italian economy for war
  (pages 85–6).

However, you will also need to explain that Mussolini's economic and
foreign policies were certainly not fully co-ordinated. In fact, several
of his foreign policy ventures had little or nothing to do with
economic factors – the intervention in the Spanish Civil war, for
example. Furthermore, when his foreign policy took Italy into the
Second World War the economy was very ill prepared for such a
conflict. Here you should refer to:

- Adverse impact of wars in Ethiopia and Spain on government
  finances (pages 85–6).
- Failure of autarky to prepare economy for the Second World War
  (pages 85–6).

Don't forget that you need to have an overall judgement about the
inter-relationship of economic and foreign policies and should
directly answer 'to what extent', i.e. fully, partially, scarcely at all.

In the style of Edexcel

'Mussolini's foreign policy in the 1930s failed to make Italy "great, respected and feared".' How far do you agree with this view?   (60 marks)

Exam tips

The cross-references are intended to take you straight to the material that will help you to answer the question.

In the exam you must take at least five minutes to plan an answer to a multi-stranded question such as this.

Begin your planning by trying to define what Mussolini meant by 'great, respected, and feared'. 'Great' for example refers to his desire to make Italy a major European power, the dominant power in the Mediterranean, and the owner of a large colonial empire (page 111).

Once you have explained what Mussolini meant, you need to assess the extent to which he achieved each of these goals. For example, under the heading of 'Respected' you should include:

- Evidence that Britain and France did or did not consider Italy a great power, on a par with themselves, e.g. Hoare–Laval Pact, Munich conference (pages 119, 121–8).

Under the heading of 'Feared' you should consider:

- The extent to which Italy became a great military power, feared by other states (pages 125–8).

It is vital that you write a strong conclusion. Here you might examine which states respected and feared Italy, and which did not. You might also consider whether Italy was more deserving of the phrase 'great, respected, and feared' at different times during the 1930s. Alternatively, is it possible to argue that Italy was 'respected' but not 'feared', or 'feared' but not 'great'?

---

9 The Second World War and the Fall of Mussolini

> **POINTS TO CONSIDER**
>
> The Second World War was to bring about the destruction of the Fascist state and the death of Mussolini. The war revealed the inefficiency and incompetence of the regime, and exposed the fragility of public support for the *Duce*. This chapter examines these themes under the following headings:
>
> * Italy in the Second World War
> * The fall of Mussolini
> * Armistice and Civil War
> * Death of Mussolini
> * Aftermath: Italy in 1945

Key dates

1940	June	Italy entered the Second World War
	September	Italian invasion of Egypt
	October	Italian invasion of Greece
1941	April	Defeat of Italian forces in East Africa
1942	October	Retreat of Axis forces from Egypt
1943	January	Libya abandoned by Italian forces
	July	Allied invasion of Sicily
	July 25	Dismissal and arrest of Mussolini
	September 8	Italy signed armistice with Allies
	September 12	Mussolini freed from prison by Germans
	September 15	Mussolini proclaimed new Fascist state – 'Italian Social Republic'
1943–5		Civil war in German-occupied northern Italy
1945	April 28	Execution of Mussolini by Italian anti-Fascists
	June	First post-war government set up
	November	Christian Democrats began dominance of post-war Italian governments

1 | Italy in the Second World War

Military unpreparedness

Key question
Why did Fascist Italy
suffer military defeats
1940–3?

Despite all Mussolini's talk of war in the years leading up to 1940
there had been no concerted effort on the part of the *Duce* or his
military leaders to prepare Italy for a sustained war. Mussolini
joined the war only when he thought Britain and France were on
the verge of utter defeat. He expected the war to be over by
September 1940 and observed that Italy needed 'a few thousand
dead to be able to attend the peace conference as a belligerent'.
As the war dragged on beyond 1940 and Britain refused to sue
for peace, the extent of Italian lack of preparedness became
painfully apparent.

Large sums had been spent on rearmament – in the period
1935–8 Italy spent 11.8 per cent of national income on armed
forces, compared to 12.9 per cent in Germany, 6.9 per cent in
France and 5.5 per cent in Britain – but much of this money had
been squandered on purchasing inadequate weaponry and on
providing luxurious living quarters for officers. The airforce, for
example, possessed only 1000 effective planes with which to 'blot
out the sun' and these were also of inferior quality – the main
fighter aircraft, the Fiat CR42 biplane, was slow and under-armed,

The much-vaunted Fascist airforce.

and was grounded in large numbers during the North African campaigns for want of sand filters for the engines.

The army was also outdated. Mussolini claimed that he had 'eight million bayonets' ready for service, but in June 1940 fewer than 800,000 men were ready to fight and these were largely equipped with rifles and artillery dating back to the First World War. Above all, the Italian army was lacking in tanks. The Second World War was to be a mechanised war but, in 1940, Italy possessed only about 1500 armoured cars and light tanks.

Key dates

Italy entered the Second World War: June 1940

Italian invasion of Egypt: September 1940

Invasion of Greece: October 1940

Inadequate leadership

The Italian soldier was not only poorly equipped, he was also poorly trained and badly led. The generals, of whom there were over 600, were steeped in the defensive traditions of the First World War and were sceptical of armoured warfare and air support. As for the navy, probably the best equipped of the three services, its admirals were reluctant to risk their new battleships against the British Mediterranean fleet, and adopted a defensive strategy throughout the war. It was largely Mussolini's fault that the military leadership was incompetent. He concentrated power in his own hands, making all the key strategic decisions on which countries to attack, and promoted officers more for their obedience and powers of flattery than for their military expertise.

Economic weakness

Despite the pre-war policy of encouraging autarky, the Italian economy was far from self-sufficient in 1940. To make matters worse, the regime had given little thought to the problem of large-scale armaments production during wartime. Strategic materials, notably coal and iron ore, had to be imported from Germany and German-occupied territories. As the war began to go badly for the Axis, the Germans became increasingly reluctant to divert such scarce resources to their ineffectual Italian allies. This led to a fall of 20 per cent in Italian steel production between 1940 and 1942 with the result that losses, particularly in tanks and aircraft, could not be replaced. Food production also fell. The wheat harvest dropped by 1.5 million tonnes as a result of many peasant farmers being drafted into the army.

Military defeats

In September 1940, Mussolini launched his campaign to expand the Italian empire in North Africa (see the map on page 124). Italian forces in Libya attacked British positions in Egypt. Not content with this, the *Duce* opened a new front in the Balkans in the following month when the Italian army in Albania invaded Greece. The Italian army, however, did not have the resources to fight two campaigns simultaneously and both offensives rapidly ground to a halt. By the end of the year the Fascist armies had been pushed back into Libya and Albania, respectively. The navy fared no better, losing half its battle fleet to a British air attack on the port of Taranto in November.

Hopes of military glory on the cheap were now fading. Britain still controlled Egypt and most of the Mediterranean, and had thwarted German plans to invade across the English Channel. The *Duce*, nevertheless, remained confident of ultimate victory. His Nazi ally, however, lacked faith in Italian arms. In February 1941 Mussolini was persuaded, reluctantly, to accept the German General Rommel as Axis commander in North Africa. In April, German armies finally ended the stalemate in the Balkans, sweeping through Yugoslavia and defeating Greece in little more than a week.

The Axis powers appeared to be winning, but it was becoming increasingly clear that Italy was not just a junior partner to Germany but also a subservient one. Italy relied on Germany for raw materials, particularly coal, and found that the crucial political and military decisions were taken by the Germans, usually without any consultation. Mussolini resented this dependency but could do little about it. The loss of Italy's East African empire to British troops in April 1941 was final proof of its military failure. The *Duce* managed to send 200,000 soldiers to the Russian front, but these men were too poorly trained and equipped to be of real value. If Italy was to gain anything at all from the war it would be through German success not its own, while German defeat would bring down Italian Fascism with it.

In 1942 there were some modest Axis successes in Russia and North Africa, but by the end of the year the Germans were on the brink of catastrophic defeat at Stalingrad and Rommel's forces in North Africa were in full retreat. Libya was abandoned to the British in January 1943 and by May the whole Axis army in North Africa had surrendered. Two months later the Anglo-American forces landed in Sicily. The invasion of the Italian mainland itself was imminent.

Defeat of Italian forces in East Africa: April 1941

Axis forces retreat from Egypt: October 1942

Italian forces abandon Libya: January 1943

Key dates

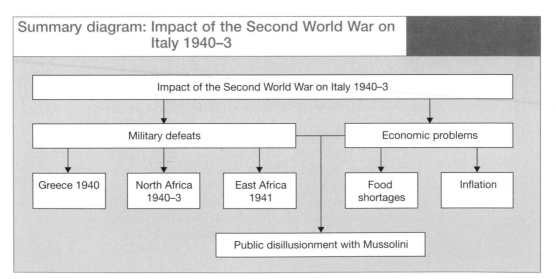

Summary diagram: Impact of the Second World War on Italy 1940–3

Key question
Why did Mussolini fall
from power?

2 | The Fall of Mussolini

Public disillusionment

Public opinion had been divided over the decision to enter the war in June 1940. There had been many doubters, but a significant number of Italians had hoped for a quick and profitable victory. Defeats in Greece and Egypt had soon destroyed such optimism. Those Italians who had believed the Fascist propaganda about an army of eight million bayonets and an airforce that could 'blot out the sun' became particularly disillusioned when they witnessed the organisational chaos, the antiquated weaponry and the lack of battle training. Soldiers home on leave recounted how the attack on Greece had begun at the start of the rainy season and how, once winter set in, the army provided only totally inadequate winter clothing. Veterans of the North African campaign described the desperate shortage of armoured vehicles.

Italian civilians, in any case, did not need to be told about Fascism's lack of preparedness for a prolonged war – they could see the evidence all around them. Food became short as grain imports fell – the result of British naval blockade in the Mediterranean – and, since the government refused to introduce rationing, prices rose dramatically. Coffee, petrol and soap became virtually unobtainable, except for those rich enough to afford the inflated prices on the flourishing black market. Eventually, in 1941, rationing was introduced, but by then stocks had run very low. Supplies were scarce and badly organised and ordinary Italians were faced with a bread ration of only 150 grams per person per day – the lowest of any combatant country except the USSR.

By the end of 1940 the Italian public was heartily sick of the war. Their faith in the *Duce*'s infallibility had been shattered. There was no longer any interest in the possible spoils of war, particularly as it was becoming increasingly apparent that further fighting would only increase German control over the country. The years 1941 and 1942 only increased the disillusionment of the Italian public, as defeat followed defeat, shortages worsened and working hours lengthened. Opposition groups, from Communist to Catholic, began to emerge. These groups were still small and disorganised but, in early 1943, shortages and anti-war sentiment led to a wave of strikes in Italian industry.

Dismissal of Mussolini

The regime was well aware of the deep unpopularity of the war and the growing contempt for the *Duce*. By late 1942 major industrialists and even prominent Fascists, notably Dino Grandi and Galeazzo Ciano, the dictator's own son-in-law, were inclined to make peace. Their realisation that Mussolini would not contemplate this, and that the Allies would not negotiate with him anyway, led them to the belief that the *Duce* must go. He could be a sacrifice or a scapegoat, peace could be arranged, and the Fascists might keep at least some of their power. Such views were echoed by conservatives at the court of King Victor Emmanuel, and among the leading generals, who feared a collapse of social order and perhaps even a Communist revolution.

The Allied conquest of Sicily in July 1943 was the final straw – the mainland was in danger of invasion and utter defeat appeared inevitable. A group of senior Fascists led by Roberto Farinacci, the ex-squad leader, and De Bono, a Fascist general in the Ethiopian campaign, persuaded Mussolini to call a meeting of the Grand Council of Fascism to discuss the military situation. The Grand Council, which had not sat since 1939, met on the night of 24–25 July 1943 and voted 19–7 to ask the King to restore all those powers to parliament, ministers and the Grand Council that Mussolini had taken away. In effect, they were seeking a way to get rid of the *Duce*, make peace, and save, if not the regime, then at least themselves.

Allied invasion of Sicily: July 1943

Dismissal and arrest of Mussolini: 25 July 1943

Key dates

The members of the Grand Council had expected a spirited defence, and even physical violence, from Mussolini and they were surprised to see the dictator subdued, perhaps ill. He could not bring himself to protest. But by the morning of 25 July the *Duce* had recovered himself and he visited the King, intending to name new ministers, punish those who had voted against him, and continue the war. However, the King, encouraged by the events of the previous night and spurred on by the army high command, told Mussolini that he was now the 'most hated man in Italy'. He declared that the war was lost and that Marshal Badoglio would take over as Prime Minister with a brief to make peace. The *Duce* was then arrested.

With the dismissal of Mussolini, the Fascist regime collapsed. There were no public protests, only public relief. Fascists, far from attempting to restore the *Duce* by calling supporters into the streets, meekly accepted the change in government. Leading Fascists tried to ingratiate themselves with the new Prime Minister. Even the Fascist mouthpiece, the *Popolo d'Italia*, simply replaced Mussolini's photograph on the front page with that of Marshal Badoglio. It had been a bloodless coup.

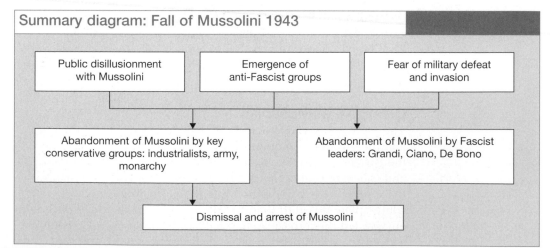

Summary diagram: Fall of Mussolini 1943

Public disillusionment with Mussolini

Emergence of anti-Fascist groups

Fear of military defeat and invasion

Abandonment of Mussolini by key conservative groups: industrialists, army, monarchy

Abandonment of Mussolini by Fascist leaders: Grandi, Ciano, De Bono

Dismissal and arrest of Mussolini

Key question
What were the
consequences of the
fall of Mussolini's
regime?

Key dates

Civil war in northern
Italy: 1943–5

Italy signed armistice
with Allies: 8
September 1943

Mussolini freed from
prison by Germans:
12 September 1943

Mussolini proclaimed
new Fascist state, the
'Italian Social
Republic': 15
September 1943

Key term

**Italian Social
Republic**
Mussolini's Fascist
regime in northern
Italy 1943–5.

3 | Armistice and Civil War

Marshal Badoglio arranged an armistice with Britain and the
USA on 8 September 1943, but it was Italy's misfortune that this
did not bring peace. Nazi Germany could not afford to let this
'backdoor' to Europe fall into Allied hands and promptly
occupied northern and central Italy. Hitler, informed that the
fallen *Duce* was being imprisoned in a ski resort in the Appenine
mountains, ordered his rescue. In a daring mission, German
troops landed by glider, seized Mussolini from his Italian captors
and crammed him into a small two-seater plane. Transferred first
to a German airbase in Italy, Mussolini was flown on to Germany
to meet Hitler. Greeting the *Führer*, Mussolini is reputed to have
declared, 'I am here to receive my orders'.

On 15 September 1943 Mussolini announced the creation of a
new German-sponsored Fascist state, the '**Italian Social
Republic**'. This new Fascist regime, heavily reliant on German
arms, controlled only a relatively small area of northern Italy. It
lacked any real public support and was rejected by those
conservative groups, notably industrialists and the Church, who
had largely embraced the pre-war Fascist state. Mussolini's
supporters were confined to pro-German Fascists such as
Farinacci, anti-Semites, and opportunists looking for wealth and
some share of power.

Mussolini being escorted onto a German plane after his rescue from prison by German troops.

The new Fascist republic lacked a capital city, any coherent structure of government and an army, but it did spawn a brutal militia. The militia groups owed allegiance to local Fascist leaders rather than the *Duce*. Acting as no more than gangsters they murdered and terrorised suspected opponents, and extorted money from local businesses. Mussolini indulged his own taste for violence by wreaking vengeance on those Grand Council members who had voted against him: Ciano and De Bono were shot in 1944.

In response to the new Fascist state and its brutality, resistance grew among a range of anti-Fascist groups, from the Catholics to Liberals and Communists. **Partisans**, often Communists or from the new, moderate Action Party, took up arms and fought against the Fascist militia. Northern Italy fell into a bloody civil war.

Partisans
Armed anti-Fascist groups.

Key term

Summary diagram: Italy 1943–5

Second World War in Italy 1943–5

- Armistice ends fighting between Italian and Anglo-American forces
- German forces occupy northern and central Italy
- Anglo-American armies slowly fight their way northwards through Italy, facing determined German resistance

Civil war in Italy 1943–5

- Fascist Italian Social Republic set up in northern Italy
- Emergence of anti-Fascist groups – Catholic, Socialist, Communist
- Fighting between Fascist militia, supported by German forces, and anti-Fascist partisans

---

4 | Death of Mussolini

During 1943–4 British and US forces slowly pushed their way northwards. By the beginning of 1945 the Nazi forces in Italy were in full retreat towards the Austrian border. Mussolini, surrounded by a dwindling band of supporters, tried to flee. On 25 April he joined a group of German soldiers heading for Austria and disguised himself in a German uniform. At Dongo on Lake Garda the group was stopped by Italian Communist partisans. The *Duce* was recognised. He and his mistress, Clara Petacci, were executed by the partisans on 28 April, their bodies taken to Milan and put on public display, strung up by the heels from the roof of a petrol station in Piazzale Loreto. It was a humiliating and ignominious end for a *Duce* once hailed as a 'Titan', a 'Genius' and even the 'Sun god' by his Fascist admirers.

Execution of Mussolini by Italian anti-Fascists: 28 April 1945

Key date

Key dates

First post-war government: June 1945

Christian Democrats begin dominance of post-war Italian governments: November 1945

5 | Aftermath: Italy in 1945

As the war ended there were revenge killings and executions, notably of the former party secretaries, Starace and Farinacci, but there was no bloodbath. In June 1945, the various anti-Fascist groups set up the first free government of Italy since 1922. This was a coalition government under the leadership of Ferruccio Parri, a resistance hero, and included his own Action Party, together with Socialists, Communists and Christian Democrats. However, Parri's party proved too small to dominate the coalition and, in November 1945, he was replaced as Prime Minister by Alcide De Gasperi of the Christian Democrats. The Christian Democrats, successors of the Catholic *Popolari* and drawing support from the middle classes and business, would dominate the new democratic Italy for the next 40 years.

The bodies of Mussolini and Clara Petacci on public display in Milan's Piazzale Loreto.

Study Guide: AS Question

In the style of OCR

Assess the impact of the Second World War on Italy to 1945.

(45 marks)

Source: OCR, January 2003

Exam tips

The cross-references are intended to take you straight to the material that will help you to answer the question.

You should avoid writing a narrative, simply telling the story of Italy in the Second World War. Instead, you should first assess the impact of the war on Italy up to the overthrow of Mussolini, and should include:

- Military defeats (pages 135–6).
- Economic impact, such as food shortages (page 137).
- The impact of military defeats and economic hardship on public attitudes towards the war and Mussolini's regime (pages 137–8).
- How the factors above convinced powerful conservative groups and key Fascist leaders to dispense with Italy (pages 137–8).

Do spell out the importance of the war in the downfall of the Fascist regime. The second part of your answer should focus on the period after Mussolini's dismissal as Prime Minister in 1943, and should include:

- The destructive impact of Mussolini's 'Italian Social Republic' and the civil war.
- The emergence of anti-Fascist groups.

In your conclusion you should identify and explain the most significant effects of the war on Italy, its politics, its economy and its society.

Glossary

Acerbo law   Mussolini's reform of elections to guarantee a Fascist victory.

Anarchists   Opposed both a strong central government and capitalism, arguing that political and economic power should be held by workers and peasants, organised at a local level.

Annex   Take over or seize a country.

Anschluss   Union between Germany and Austria, which had been prohibited by the Treaty of Versailles.

Anti-clericalism   Many Liberals were anti-clerical in the sense that they opposed the intrusion of the Catholic Church into politics. For example, they did not want Catholicism to be declared the official religion of Italy, and advocated civil rather than religious marriage ceremonies.

Anti-clericals   Those politicians, mainly Liberal, who opposed the claims of the Catholic Church that it deserved a privileged position within the Italian state.

Anti-imperialist   Opposition to expanding Italy's empire.

Anti-Semitism   Hatred of Jews.

Armistice   Agreement to cease fighting.

Autarky   Economic self-sufficiency allowing a country to operate without importing food or other key materials from other countries.

Authoritarian state   A state with a strong central government that is able and willing to ignore parliament and suppress dissent.

Aventine secession   Anti-Fascist MPs walked out of parliament in protest against Fascist violence, hoping that this would encourage the King to sack Mussolini.

Balkans   Area of south-eastern Europe including Greece, Albania and Yugoslavia.

Ballot-rigging   Fixing the result of an election by such illegal measures as destroying votes cast for opposition parties or adding fraudulent voting papers.

Battle for Grain   Fascism's attempt to make Italy self-sufficient in the production of grain, and thus bread.

Blackshirts   Armed Fascist militia.

Blitzkrieg   'Lightning war' tactics employed by Nazis very successfully in the the early years of the Second World War. Involved co-ordinated use of aircraft, tanks and infantry.

Bolshevik   Term for Communists.

Bourgeoisie   The middle classes, owners of businesses.

Chamber of Deputies   The lower, but most important, house in the Italian parliament – similar to the British House of Commons.

Civil service   Civil servants advise government ministers on policy and ensure that government policies are carried out.

Collectivisation   Seizure of private land by the state. The land would then be re-organised into state-run farms or distributed to groups of peasants.

Confindustria   A powerful, conservative organisation representing big businesses.

Constitutional monarchy   The King was the head of state but the Prime Minister was the head of the government. The King had the power to dismiss Prime Ministers but in practice left day-to-day politics in the hands of the Prime Minister and parliament. To stay in office and to pass new laws the Prime Minister needed the approval of the elected parliament.

Corporate state   Every industry would be part of a Fascist-led corporation that would sort out disputes between workers and management, and help to organise production, pay and conditions.

Coup d'état   The violent overthrow of the government.

Depression   A period of economic stagnation that began in the USA and affected all European industrialised countries for most of the 1930s.

Duce   All-powerful leader. This was Mussolini's self-attributed 'title', which the regime encouraged people to use. It signified that he was not just Prime Minister, but also the effective dictator of Italy.

Economic sanctions   To pressurise Italy into seeking a peaceful solution to the Ethiopian crisis, the League banned trade with Italy in certain goods such as grain, steel and textiles. However, the ban did not include oil, the one commodity that would have damaged the Italian war effort.

Entente powers   The Alliance of Britain, France and Russia (Triple Entente).

Establishment   The political, economic and military élite who traditionally held power in a country.

Free trade unions   Trade unions which represented the interests of workers, and which were independent of government or Fascist control.

Grand Council of Fascism   The supreme body within the Fascist movement, which discussed policy proposals and made all key appointments within the Fascist Party.

Hoare–Laval Pact   An Anglo-French attempt to find a compromise peace, giving Mussolini most of Ethiopia.

Italian Social Republic   Mussolini's Fascist regime in northern Italy 1943–5.

Lateran Agreements   These comprised a treaty and a deal, known as a concordat, which officially ended the dispute about the role and status of the Catholic Church in the Italian state.

League of Nations   International organisation of over 100 countries designed to help to prevent wars and end disputes between countries.

Leggi Fascistissime   All opposition parties and organisations banned.

Liberal historian   A historian who sympathises with the Liberal regime, arguing that Italy, prior to Fascism, was maturing into a stable, parliamentary democracy.

Marxist historian   A historian who broadly subscribes to the views of Karl Marx. Marxist historians argue that Liberal regimes are a guise for the exploitation of the working class and that such regimes will be overthrown once the working class realise and exert their political strength.

'Mussolini made the trains run on time'   This phrase was coined by foreign journalists to suggest that the Fascist regime had somehow improved the efficiency of Italian industries.

Mutilated victory   The claim that Italy had been denied its rightful territorial gains in the peace settlement after the First World War.

National Fascist Party   Set up by Mussolini to unite the Fascist movement and to increase his control over local Fascist squads and their leaders.

National militia   Fascist squads were converted into a national militia, giving them legal status. This blackshirted militia was under Fascist Party control.

OVRA   Fascist secret police.

Partisans   Armed anti-Fascist groups.

Patronage   The use of appointments and promotions to reward support.

Polarising   Moving towards extremes.

Popolari   Catholic political party founded in January 1919.

Press censorship   Newspapers were no longer permitted to criticise the Fascist government.

Proletariat   Industrial working class.

Ras   Local Fascist leaders, usually with their own Fascist squads.

Reactionary   Hostile to parliamentary or democratic government, dismissive of individual freedoms, deeply suspicious of change.

Republicans   Wanted to abolish the monarchy.

Revaluation   The Fascist government tried to increase the value of the lira against other countries' currencies.

Revisionist   A state that wanted to change the peace treaties signed after the First World War.

Roman question   The question of the role of the Catholic Church in the Italian state, including the territorial claims of the Pope over Rome, the issues of civil and church marriage and divorce.

Satellite state   A country that is very heavily influenced or virtually controlled by another state.

Socialist   Socialists argued that the existing political and economic systems of Europe oppressed the poor. Socialists worked to improve the political and economic status of the working class. Some believed the existing political systems could be reformed peacefully, others argued that only violent revolution could bring about meaningful change.

Sphere of influence   An area where Italy would be the dominant power.

Squadrismo   The violent attacks of Fascist gangs, or squads.

Status quo   The current or existing situation.

Sudetenland   The area of Czechoslovakia with a substantial German-speaking population. Hitler used this as a pretext to wage war against the Western European powers.

Tariffs   Taxes placed on imports of foreign products.

Trasformismo   Different political factions forming a coalition government regardless of ideological differences.

Triple Alliance   Military alliance between Italy, Germany and Austria-Hungary signed in 1882.

Two-party system   A political system, as in Britain, where there are two dominant and distinct parties who compete for power.

Universal manhood suffrage   The right to vote for all men over the age of 21.

Vatican City   The area of Rome, comprising St Peter's, the Papal apartments and the offices of the Papal bureaucracy, which was ruled directly by the Pope and was completely independent from the Italian state.

War of attrition   A war in which the commanders do not expect dramatic victories but instead measure success in terms of metres of territory gained and number of enemy killed.

Index